Dan Gookin's

PC
Hotline

Dan Gookin's

PC Hotline

DAN GOOKIN

PUBLISHED BY
Microsoft Press
A Division of Microsoft Corporation
One Microsoft Way
Redmond, Washington 98052-6399

Library of Congress Cataloging-in-Publication Data
Gookin, Dan.
    [PC hotline]
    Dan Gookin's PC hotline / Dan Gookin.
       p.   cm.
    Includes index.
    ISBN 1-55615-473-9
    1. Microcomputers--Maintenance and repair.   I. Title.   II. Title:
PC hotline.
TK7887.G66   1992
004.2'56--dc20   92-4432
                                                          CIP

Printed and bound in the United States of America.

1 2 3 4 5 6 7 8 9   RDRD   6 5 4 3 2 1

Distributed to the book trade in Canada by Macmillan of Canada, a division of
Canada Publishing Corporation.

Distributed to the book trade outside the United States and Canada by Penguin
Books Ltd.

Penguin Books Ltd., Harmondsworth, Middlesex, England
Penguin Books Australia Ltd., Ringwood, Victoria, Australia
Penguin Books N.Z. Ltd., 182-190 Wairau Road, Auckland 10, New Zealand

British Cataloging-in-Publication Data available.

Mac® and Macintosh® are registered trademarks of Apple Computer, Inc. Intel® is a
registered trademark and Above™ is a trademark of Intel Corporation. AT®, IBM®, and
PS/2® are registered trademarks of International Business Machines Corporation.
Microsoft®, MS®, MS-DOS®, and XENIX® are registered trademarks and Windows™ is
a trademark of Microsoft Corporation. OS/2® is a registered trademark licensed to
Microsoft Corporation.

Aquisitions Editor: Mike Halvorson
Project Editor: Sally Brunsman
Technical Editor: Dail Magee, Jr.
Editing and Production: Online Press Inc.

Contents

Acknowledgments

Once again I'm blessed to be producing a book with Microsoft Press, a group of people who would be fun and exciting to work with even without all the coffee, beer, free pop, and the cool cafeteria in Building 16.

Special thanks go to: Mike Halvorson, "the defector" (favorite night on the town: "Black juice and Bothar hunting"); Sally Brunsman, the red-pencil-on-blue-sticky-notes lady (favorite quote: "It's his style"); Dail "I'm not from Utah anymore!" Magee, Jr., owner of the coolest Windows system at Microsoft and Post-it Tape Flag color coordinator; Joyce Cox and all the nice people at Online Press—Polly Urban, Christina Smith, and Zaafar Hasnain—who did their job so well I have nothing silly to say about them; Margarite Hargrave for the graphics, and Jim Brown for again trusting me at the keyboard (uh-huh). And special thanks to David "LAN Man" Rygmyr for appreciating my Novell key chain gift.

Special thanks also go to: Matt Wagner of Waterside Productions; Sandra for the love; and Jordan for sticking Batman in my eye when I was sick. Extraneous thanks go to: the government of California for helping me in my decision to move out of the state; and the Swedish Bikini Team who, if anything, bring us the message that, yes, things can get better.

Introduction

Your PC is bursting with untapped potential, and unlocking that potential is what this book is all about. This isn't easy to accept. If you have fast equipment, you probably assume your computer is running at top speed. You've paid for it, and that's the way it is. Even so, your "fast" equipment can be made to work even faster. And if you think you have slow equipment, stand by for your PC's wake-up call!

Just telling you how to improve your PC's performance isn't enough. We also have to tackle the subject everyone avoids: things that can go wrong.

PCs work flawlessly most of the time. Yet because we rely on them for so much, even the smallest electronic burp can lead to great anxiety. Not to worry; every problem has a solution, and this book tells you how to prevent catastrophe and how to deal with mishaps if they occur. I've brought together ways to make your PC run more efficiently and ways to solve problems—giving you a personal *PC Hotline*.

UNLOCKING YOUR PC'S POWER

This book provides all you need to know to improve your PC's performance and solve common problems. How? By using the MS-DOS operating system, which provides all the tools necessary to make your PC run more efficiently, improve responsiveness, and recover from any mishaps.

Boosting performance, safeguarding data, recovering from disaster, and troubleshooting are all possible using only MS-DOS. This book shows you how to do the following:

■ Organize your files, which makes you work smarter and makes MS-DOS work more efficiently

■ Create *super MS-DOS commands*, which are smarter than standard MS-DOS commands and capable of doing things MS-DOS cannot do

■ Augment MS-DOS using special utilities you create with Debug

- Improve the speed of your hardware and boost disk performance
- Work with memory, making more of it available for MS-DOS and your applications
- Protect your valuable files and data from accidental deletion and viral infection
- Recover from disaster

All this could be done automatically. However, MS-DOS needs to be flexible. Fifty million PC users do things fifty million different ways. MS-DOS must be accommodating, so it makes no assumptions about how *you* want to accomplish a particular task. It's up to you to discover what MS-DOS can do and apply it to your situation.

IS THIS BOOK FOR YOU?

I've deliberately written this book in a nontechnical and friendly manner. Nothing it contains is difficult but, at the same time, this isn't a beginner's book. If you're just starting out, I recommend that you read Van Wolverton's *Running MS-DOS*, also from Microsoft Press. If you already know what an MS-DOS prompt is and consider yourself fairly proficient at using MS-DOS commands, then you're ready for this book.

The only other requirements for using this book are that you're an MS-DOS user and have a PC and applications to run. This book assumes that you have a hard-disk drive; if you don't, you should upgrade. Finally, this book uses commands from MS-DOS 5. If you don't yet have version 5, I recommend upgrading.

HOW TO USE THIS BOOK

This book covers three major themes: boosting performance, or using MS-DOS to improve the way you work; protecting your data and performing preventive maintenance; and recovering from disaster.

Feel free to start reading anywhere. You can even read from front to back if you like. Chapter 5 contains information about creating the *Emergency Boot Disk*, which is referenced in several other chapters. You might want to start with Chapter 5, especially if you see trouble looming on the horizon.

To help you decide where to start, these are the topics listed by chapter:

- Chapter 1 provides an overview of why your PC is imperfect and how you can make it "more perfect."

- Chapter 2 covers working with files and organizing your hard disk.

- Chapter 3 shows you how to augment MS-DOS using super MS-DOS commands, batch files, and special utilities written with Debug.

- Chapter 4 tells you how to fine-tune your system.

- Chapter 5 begins the discussion of preventive maintenance by showing you how to create an Emergency Boot Disk.

- Chapter 6 discusses what to do to prevent system crashes and shows you ways to protect your data.

- Chapter 7 concentrates on hardware problems: how to locate them, and whether to repair or replace defective parts.

- Chapter 8 deals with disasters and gives recovery steps for specific PC emergencies.

- Chapter 9 presents the problem of the computer virus: how to prevent it, detect it, and remove it.

- Chapter 10 discusses third-party utilities that are designed to boost performance, protect data, and help you recover from mishaps.

- Chapter 11 is your one-step troubleshooting guide.

- Appendixes A, B, and C offer a handy system configuration checklist and summary information about error messages and the Emergency Boot Disk.

SUMMARY

This book shows you how to get more power from your PC and, in the process, make your PC's environment safer and more reliable. In the rare chance that disaster does strike, this book also tells you what to do and how to avoid the problem in the future. Good luck, and get ready for your introduction to a more powerful PC.

Chapter 1

Making Your PC As Perfect As Possible

How can your PC be more perfect? Let me count the ways: It can work faster. It can help you work more effectively. It can better protect files from inadvertent deletion or from being accidentally stomped on. It can be made safer, protecting vital files and areas of the hard disk against a dreaded *crash* and giving your system a longer, happier life. Bad things do happen to a PC, but it's possible to prevent some problems and make the effects of others less disastrous.

This chapter discusses what can go wrong with your PC. Disasters can strike, but more often, your system's performance is degraded as a result of neglect. The rest of this book discusses what you can do to prevent disaster and how you can avoid degraded performance.

WHAT CAN GO WRONG

Lots of things can go wrong in a computer. No sense in rattling off the whole list—you probably know most of the problems by heart (and had nightmares about the rest). But what exactly goes wrong? It depends.

The most common problem PC users face is performance degradation. This happens to any system just by using it. (Witness the Byzantine Empire or any communist bureaucracy.) For example, your hard disk may become cluttered with files. The result is a disorganized system that slows down both you and MS-DOS; it takes you longer to find files, and it makes MS-DOS work harder to manage the mess.

Performance can also be diminished simply by not taking advantage of what MS-DOS has to offer. MS-DOS is full of tricks. Some of the best tricks go unused, however, because users are unaware of them or are

afraid to try them. The end result is that your system doesn't shine as
brightly as it could.

Boosting performance is positive; avoiding it can be negative. Beyond
losing its edge, your PC can be subject to seemingly random and self-
inflicted acts of destruction, which in turn lead to what's known as the
system crash.

Crash is a drastic term. It has direct ties to aviation, where it's applied in
the most ugly of circumstances. In computers, a crash refers to what happens when a hard-disk drive's read/write heads make contact with the disk
surface; due to the great speeds involved, the heads actually crash into the
disk, spewing splinters of aluminum and magnetic oxide dust. (Hackers
refer to this as *farming.*) A crash typically renders the hard disk and all its
data useless and is definitely something to avoid if you can. More generally, the term *crash* applies to any time the system doesn't work right.

Different degrees of problems can occur inside a computer, and not all of
them lead to disaster. What's important is your data, primarily the files on
your hard disk. As long as you take the proper steps to protect your data,
you can survive any potential mishap.

Why Bad Things Happen

Things run amok in a computer when something that is meant to happen
doesn't. How your computer responds will vary. In cases of performance
degradation, you can continue using the computer unaware that it's not
running up to par. For minor problems, you will receive error messages. If
the computer crashes, you can reset the computer (or turn it off and on
again), and everything will be back to normal. What caused the problem?
Who knows—maybe phases of the moon, the programmer's mood, or
cosmic rays.

Seriously, most PC problems fall into one of these four categories:

■ Problems with MS-DOS

■ Problems with applications

■ Problems with hardware

■ Nasty things: viruses and their ilk

The following sections elaborate on these categories, telling you how each can contribute to PC problems.

Problems with MS-DOS

MS-DOS is your computer's operating system, the main program in charge of everything on the PC. Being such a key element of the system means that MS-DOS can quickly bring the computer to its knees under certain circumstances.

When it comes to managing files on disk, MS-DOS is fairly proficient. It provides all the tools necessary to get the job done, and what MS-DOS can't do, third-party programs can handle with ease.

Most of the time, MS-DOS isn't to blame for a system crash. MS-DOS tries its best to stay alive and, for the most part, it remains pretty solid. There really isn't such a thing as an MS-DOS crash, but you can do things with MS-DOS that can lead to anything from a hiccup to a major crash.

Some MS-DOS accidents have really boneheaded causes. The infamous *Bad command or file name* error message is simply MS-DOS's way of telling you that it doesn't understand what you typed at the prompt. This isn't a crash at all. Luckily, MS-DOS can deal with most of these situations and simply informs you of a goof by giving an error message.

On a higher level, MS-DOS has what are called *fatal errors*. These occur when MS-DOS tries to do something and the computer responds in an unexpected manner. Despite the word *fatal*, nothing is out of control, and your blood pressure need not rise. The fatal error is earmarked by the telltale prompt *Abort, Retry, Ignore, Fail?*

Other common problems with MS-DOS include missing files (the *File not found* error message is displayed); typos in your CONFIG.SYS or AUTOEXEC.BAT files that can halt the computer until you correct them; and other minor blunders. All can be easily mended.

Problems with Applications

Software can help you get your work done—or it can slow you down if it doesn't behave properly. Demanding programs, and especially programs that circumvent MS-DOS to get things done "more efficiently," can be a source of endless trouble.

Up front, you should know that applications can produce their own array of errors. Some of these can be MS-DOS–like errors, such as *File not found*, *Disk full*, and so on. (Applications often use their own wording or, worse, cryptic codes that have no apparent meaning.) Other errors can occur with the application itself. Problems with applications can arise when files are missing or are damaged on disk by other programs or by failing hardware. If the application can handle the situation, you might see an error message. If the application can't handle the situation, the whole system may come tumbling down.

Then there's the issue of *bugs*. These are unintentional parts of an application that run haywire. Bugs exist because programming a computer is an art, not a science. Often you can tell if something works only by trying it. In a large application, developers frequently have little time to try everything, so users end up finding bugs after a product is released.

Problems with Hardware

Even if the software performs flawlessly, hardware problems can bring a computer to a screeching halt.

MS-DOS can alert you to such hardware goofs as an open disk-drive door, a printer with its power turned off, or even a flaky disk. Some problems require more attention than others, but a simple solution is often at hand: Close the disk-drive door, turn on the printer, use another disk, and so on.

Some hardware problems simply involve troubleshooting: Keyboards, monitors, and other devices can become unplugged or need cleaning. But some hardware problems require more serious measures.

Disk problems are the worst: All your data is stored on disk, so when a disk starts to get sick, you could be faced with the loss of all your files and the important information they contain. Glitchy disks and corrupted sectors can cause more worries than a letter from the IRS.

Not everything associated with hardware is an actual problem. System performance is a key issue with any computer. For example, using special techniques or buying appropriate software can help you squeeze more power from a disk drive that doesn't perform up to par. Overall, these tricks can boost performance as well as guarantee your data is safe in case something serious happens.

Nasty Things: Viruses and Their Ilk

Sometimes things can go wrong on purpose. Some heinous programs have been designed to do exactly that. These programs have clever, attention-grabbing names: Trojan horses, logic bombs, worms, and the ever-popular virus. These programs do exist, some proliferate, and they can wreak havoc on your system on purpose. But they aren't as common as the media stories about them.

The truth is that viruses aren't out to get every computer. But thanks to over-coverage by the media, it's common to think that every minor glitch is caused by a virus. Usually—thankfully—this isn't the case. A program run amok or a missing MS-DOS command is a more likely cause of any trauma. And, typically, viruses leave telltale messages that let you know you have a virus. (For details about viruses, see Chapter 9.)

WHAT YOU CAN DO

You are not powerless when it comes to dealing with a sluggish system or preventing a crash. Solutions abound for improving the way MS-DOS works. And when you can't control a situation such as a crash, there are techniques you can use to recover lost data, restore the system, and continue using your computer.

Boosting Performance

You have three ways to get more from your system: Take advantage of memory, optimize your hardware, and perform routine file maintenance and hard-disk management. These subjects are covered in this book starting with Chapter 2.

Taking advantage of memory is a big hurdle but, fortunately, one you need to clear only once. After you've set up your PC the way you like, there's no further tweaking required. Optimizing the hard drive, as well as doing other hardware performance tuning, isn't difficult. You will probably find the biggest boost in performance comes from simple file maintenance— which most people avoid like cheese-flavored ice cream. File maintenance simply means using MS-DOS file-manipulation commands to keep your system organized. A clean, neatly arranged hard disk makes MS-DOS more effective and helps you keep your data in order. File maintenance is just something you need to get in the habit of doing.

Preventing a Potential Crash

The best way to avoid a system crash is to anticipate one and try to work around it. Cars come with a spare tire for a reason. It's not that tires are flaky and tend to randomly pop. Instead, cars have spare tires in anticipation of some roadway hazard—such as that truck ahead loaded with nails and a dozing driver. Like being a defensive driver and carrying a spare tire to avoid problems on the road, there are many things you can do with your computer to prevent a system crash or deal with one if it occurs.

Preventing a crash involves using the proper tools, both hardware and software. Some programs, such as the Mirror program that comes with MS-DOS, are specifically designed as prevention tools. (The Mirror program and general prevention information are described in this book starting in Chapter 5.) If you use these tools often, they are like that spare tire sitting in your trunk, awaiting a blowout that might or might not occur.

Finally, the most important way to prevent problems is by backing up your data. I mention it last because using the MS-DOS Backup program can be a real drag. But nothing beats that emergency copy of your data; no hard-disk crash, bug, or virus can destroy it. And don't rule out the "timed backup" feature many applications have: I would have lost a whole chapter of this book if it weren't for my word-processing program's automatic backup (save) feature that saves every five minutes. If your software has an automatic backup option, use it.

Keeping Track of Your System Setup

When a problem occurs, knowing what you have inside your computer is central to figuring out what went wrong, especially when you are dealing with hardware incompatibilities and with recovery afterward. Appendix A provides a fill-in-the-blank form that you can use to record pertinent information about your computer. Fill it in as soon as you get the chance.

Another important thing to keep track of is the *CMOS memory*. On PC/AT-style computers (those with 80286 or later microprocessors), the CMOS memory, or battery–backed-up random access memory (RAM), keeps track of certain parts of your computer. If CMOS memory becomes damaged, the computer will start with an error message, and you can suddenly find that your hard disk is "missing." Finding the hard disk is easy if you have a copy of the contents of CMOS memory on paper somewhere.

Hardware Cures

If something goes wrong with your hardware, you have two choices: Fix it or replace it. Surprisingly, replacing a damaged piece of hardware is often easier—and cheaper—than getting it fixed. For the replacement, you can often select a larger, faster, and more up-to-date model. (And that never hurts anything.)

Minor repairs are sometimes possible as well: You can always tighten connections, upgrade memory, and expand your system. But generally, I recommend opting for replacing something rather than repairing it. For more information about dealing with hardware problems, see Chapter 7.

Creating the Emergency Boot Disk

To pull your computer back from the brink, keep some recovery tools handy. These tools include MS-DOS's "disaster recovery" programs, important data files, and any other programs you need to revive a computer that's in a state of shock. Of course, if the recovery programs are on your hard disk, and that's what crashed, they aren't going to do you any good. Therefore, it's a good idea to put the recovery programs all on one handy, bootable disk. I call this the *Emergency Boot Disk*.

By restarting your computer with the Emergency Boot Disk, you can get your system back up, run some diagnostic tests, and find out what happened. Then, using the proper software tools on the Emergency Boot Disk, you can start the recovery process. Thanks to the ingenious nature of modern software recovery tools, chances are good that your system will be back up and running in no time.

Creating an Emergency Boot Disk is central to the recovery processes discussed in this book. Chapter 5 explains how to set up and test the disk. Later chapters show you how to copy additional files and information to that disk. The object is to create one vital disk, full of utilities and necessary files, with which you can resuscitate an indisposed PC.

SUMMARY

Sadly, your PC isn't perfect. Hardware and software problems can occur. Even without problems, simply using a computer eventually degrades its performance. Don't lose hope, however, because this book shows you ways to anticipate and recover from system problems, as well as ways you can boost your PC's performance.

Chapter 2

Keeping Your House In Order

One fundamental rule of computing goes like this: You can keep your desk cluttered, your office a mess, papers and magazines towering sloppily toward the ceiling, but keep your PC neat and tidy. Complying with this rule requires effort and a definite plan of attack. This chapter shows you the best ways to approach hard-disk organization, how to work with your files, and how to best maintain and use a hard-disk drive.

THE RULES OF HARD-DISK MANAGEMENT

Keep your house in order. But what exactly is your house? It's your hard disk with all your programs and data files on it. Keeping that stuff organized falls under the topic of *hard-disk management*, a professional term for doing the basic chores that are a part of using MS-DOS and your PC. Hard-disk management can be summed up with three rules:

1. Organize.

2. Preserve the root directory.

3. Back up.

Each of the three rules is important. But Rule 1, Organize, is critical to running a top-flight hard disk. When you don't organize, you invite potential mishaps and encourage carelessness. And when you do organize, the other two rules naturally fall into place.

Rule 1: Organize

In MS-DOS, organization means subdirectories. You create subdirectories into which you place similar files and programs. But talking about it and making it happen are two different things. It's hard to appreciate what organization can do for you unless you have some concrete examples to follow. See the "Organizing Your Hard Disk" section on the next page.

Why bother organizing? After all, your hard disk can store megabytes of information, so who needs subdirectories? The answer is twofold: First, an organized hard disk helps you work more efficiently. (You'll read how in a minute.) Second, MS-DOS limits the number of files you can store in the root directory. Because of the way hard disks are formatted, there is room for only 512 files in the root directory of any hard disk. If you try to add a 513th file, MS-DOS gives you a *Disk full* error message—even though megabytes of space might be available on the disk!

On the other hand, MS-DOS does not limit the number of files sub-directories can store. Put a few key subdirectories off the root directory, and your hard drive can store thousands of files. (Subdirectories have a practical limit of about 512 files as well, but they can expand as necessary. Note that performance does degrade somewhat as you add more files.)

Rule 2: Preserve the Root Directory

Preserving the root directory means keeping it uncluttered. The root direc-tory is where all the other subdirectories start, like the lobby of some great building. An ideal root directory contains only a few files, primarily those that absolutely must be located in the root directory. Everything else should be in subdirectories, like elevators that take you to other floors in the building.

What must go into the root directory? MS-DOS requires only one file: COMMAND.COM. If present, CONFIG.SYS and AUTOEXEC.BAT must reside in the root directory, but MS-DOS can boot without them as long as COMMAND.COM is in the root. If you use the Shell configuration com-mand in CONFIG.SYS, you can stick COMMAND.COM in a directory other than the root, leaving CONFIG.SYS and AUTOEXEC.BAT as the only must-haves for the root. The only other items in the root directory should be subdirectories (see Figure 2-1). They branch off the root and contain programs and data files. Keeping your subdirectories tidy is the organizational part of hard-disk management.

```
Volume in drive C is MS-DOS 5
Volume Serial Number is 084C 9D22
Directory of  C:\

123          <DIR>      8-24-91    4:44p
SYSTEM       <DIR>      8-24-91    4:45p
TEMP         <DIR>      8-24-91    5:01p
WIN          <DIR>      8-24-91    5:01p
WP           <DIR>      8-24-91    4:44p
AUTOEXEC BAT      1684  7-31-91    6:54p
CONFIG   SYS       597  7-31-91    6:55p
        6 File(s)           2281 bytes
                         8853504 bytes free
```

Figure 2-1. *The minimalist's root directory.*

What about the batch files that some installation programs stick in the root directory? They're more useful in a special batch-file subdirectory, so you should move them there. And what about the data files that some programs stick in the root directory? Unfortunately, there's nothing you can do about them—unless you can tell the program to put the files elsewhere. For example, Microsoft Windows puts the WINA20.386 file in the root. You can move it elsewhere, but you must then modify the SYSTEM.INI file to tell Windows where to find WINA20.386.

Rule 3: Back Up

Back up. Do it. Refer to Chapter 6 for the details.

ORGANIZING YOUR HARD DISK

As I've said, the second rule of hard-disk management is to preserve the root directory. That means keeping it free of files and programs, which really can go elsewhere on the hard disk. Where can they go? Into subdirectories.

How you organize your hard disk depends on the applications you use and the data you create. A simple form of organization puts each of your major applications in its own subdirectory off the root: word processor, spreadsheet, database, and so on. Subdirectories can also be collective, containing many related programs: utilities, games, batch files, and so forth. And you need a subdirectory for MS-DOS. You can picture this structure like an organizational chart, as shown in Figure 2-2 on the following page.

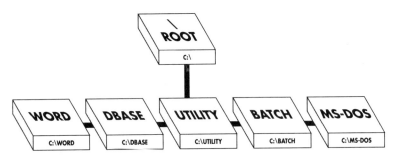

Figure 2-2. *A livable hard-disk organization.*

Most applications create their own directories when you install the programs. Some installation programs further organize applications by creating additional subdirectories. For example, Windows creates subdirectories for its system files, temporary files, and "spool" files. WordPerfect for Windows creates subdirectories for its macros, utilities, and graphics. The goal in each case is organization.

Organizing Programs

You start organizing your system by grouping similar files into directories. If an installation program doesn't do it for you, do it yourself by using MS-DOS to create subdirectories and move related files and programs into the subdirectories.

MS-DOS has three commands that let you work with subdirectories (see Table 2-1).

TABLE 2-1. MS-DOS'S DIRECTORY COMMANDS

Command	Abbreviation	Description
Mkdir	Md	Creates a new directory
Chdir	Cd	Changes to a directory or displays the name of the current directory
Rmdir	Rd	Removes a directory

For example, you start creating a collective directory for storing games with the Md (or Mkdir) command:

```
C>md \games
```

This command creates the GAMES directory under the root; the path is C:\GAMES. Your next job is to copy various games to that directory. You do this by changing to the various subdirectories where your games are kept and then copying the games one at a time to the new GAMES directory. For example, to change to the MISC\JERRY directory, where you've stashed a bunch of games given to you by a friend, you enter

```
C>cd \misc\jerry
```

To copy a game from the current directory to the new GAMES directory, you enter the following:

```
C>copy blaster.exe \games
        1 file(s) copied
```

Then you'll want to delete the original file to save space:

```
C>del blaster.exe
```

Repeat these three steps for similar files scattered all over your hard drive: Change to a subdirectory, copy the file to the correct directory, and delete the original file.

Let's say that you have a specific game subdirectory called MAHJONGG off the root. You can move that whole directory into GAMES with four MS-DOS commands: Md, Xcopy, Del, and Rd. First, create an identical subdirectory under GAMES:

```
C>md \games\mahjongg
```

Second, copy all the files and directories under MAHJONGG (the original directory) using the handy Xcopy command (which is covered in detail later in this chapter):

```
C>xcopy \mahjongg \games\mahjongg /s/e
```

Third, delete the original files and directory:

```
C>del mahjongg
All files in directory will be deleted!
Are you sure (Y/N)?
```

Enter *Y*. Then remove the original directory using the Rd command:

```
C>rd mahjongg
```

You've moved the files, and your system is now more organized. If you have additional game directories on your hard disk, you should also move them to the GAMES directory, moving subdirectories if necessary.

If you get the message *Invalid path, not directory, or directory not empty* when you try to remove the original directory, then you'll need to weave your way through the original directory, removing any files and subdirectories. You cannot use the Rd command unless a directory is completely empty. You might even have to use the Dir command with the /A switch to look for hidden files. If you find any, delete them as well, specifying their exact names. (You cannot use wildcards to delete hidden files.)

You can use this procedure to organize other types of files and subdirectories. For example, if you use more than one word processor, you can create a general WORDS directory and then move your word processors into individual subdirectories within the general directory. A general UTILITY directory is good for stashing various utility programs and subdirectories of utility programs.

Organizing Data Files

Data files should also be placed in their own subdirectories. This is an often-ignored yet important aspect of organization. For example, you could toss every file you create with your spreadsheet into a collective DATA subdirectory. But why do that, when instead you can make separate directories that organize the files based on what they are used for?

For example, consider Figure 2-3. Under the Excel directory are various subdirectories for your worksheets. Each one has a name that reflects its content, which also aids in organizing. You know that a worksheet in the PRIVATE directory is probably your own personal stuff; a worksheet stored elsewhere might belong to the company or some other department.

Note how the BUDGET directory in Figure 2-3 has its own subdirectories, one for each year. Those could be subdivided further for each month. (Nested directories are "legal" under MS-DOS.) As a result, a file in a month subdirectory could have the following pathname:

C:\EXCEL\BUDGET\1992\JUNE\MARKTING.XLS

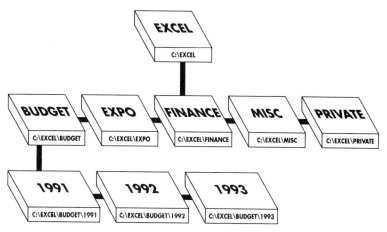

Figure 2-3. *A method of organizing data subdirectories.*

The eight-character MS-DOS filename limit doesn't seem so bad when you have organization like that. You can tell exactly what that file is about simply by its well-organized location: a Microsoft Excel spreadsheet that contains the Marketing budget for June 1992.

Also, note the MISC directory in Figure 2-3. Making a general MISC—or TEMP—directory is a good idea. It provides a place for stuffing files that just don't fit anywhere else. However, if enough similar files start showing up in your MISC directory, consider making another subdirectory for those similar files.

You can apply the type of data-file directory structure shown in Figure 2-3 to all your applications. Word processors can use it, as can database managers, graphics programs, or just about anything. Keeping your files organized is the key.

More About Creating Subdirectories

Never be afraid to create a new directory. In fact, a subdirectory with more than 512 files in it is too big. You should consider moving some of those files into another subdirectory, or better still consider *archiving* the files you're not using. (The subject of archiving is covered later in this chapter.)

Note: When MS-DOS creates a subdirectory, it has room for at least 512—and sometimes more—files. When you go beyond that number, MS-DOS creates an extension to the subdirectory, allowing it to hold more files. Although you can put more files in the subdirectory, the extension will slow down the Dir command, as well as any program that searches through the directory for a file.

Renaming Subdirectories

We've talked about Md, Cd, and Rd, the MS-DOS commands for working with directories. What's missing is a Rename command that allows you to rename a subdirectory. Under MS-DOS 5, you can use the MS-DOS Shell program to rename a directory. However, if you have MS-DOS version 2.0 or later, you can create a nifty Rendir utility to rename a subdirectory just as you would rename a file. You create this utility using the Debug program that comes with MS-DOS. First, you create a script, which is a text file containing special commands for Debug. The script for Rendir is listed in Figure 2-4. Create the script using your favorite text editor or the MS-DOS Editor. Pay close attention to the codes you enter; they must be exact. Save the text file to disk as RENDIR.SCR.

After creating RENDIR.SCR, you can build the RENDIR.COM program by entering the following command:

```
C>debug <rendir.scr
```

The RENDIR.SCR file feeds its input to Debug, and the end result is the RENDIR.COM file on disk. You can then copy RENDIR.COM to your UTILITY or BATCH directory.

Use the Rendir command to rename a directory just as you would use Ren to rename a file. (In fact, you can use Rendir to rename files as well.) The syntax for Rendir is the same as for the Ren command:

    rendir *oldname newname*

The new name for the directory must follow MS-DOS's filename rules, and it can't be a name already used by a file or subdirectory in the current directory. If you goof, Rendir displays the message *Duplicate file name or Directory not found.*

```
n rendir.com
e100 BA 3D 01 BE 5C 00 BF 71
e108 01 B9 24 00 FC F3 A4 2E
e110 80 3E 72 01 20 74 1E 2E
e118 80 3E 81 01 00 75 16 2E
e120 80 3E 82 01 20 74 0E BA
e128 6A 01 B4 17 CD 21 3C 00
e130 74 07 BA 3D 01 B4 09 CD
e138 21 B4 4C CD 21
e13D "Duplicate file name or Directory not found"
e167 0D
e168 0A 24 FF 00 00 00 00 00
e170 10
rcx
71
w
q
```

Figure 2-4. *The RENDIR.SCR Debug script file.*

If the program does not work, then you have probably mistyped a code. Double-check your script against Figure 2-4 to verify that you typed all the numbers and letters accurately. If you didn't, edit the script file and feed it into Debug again.

AVOIDING THE HULKING COW

How many files are too many? It depends. Some users fill up their hard disks like gas tanks. You really want to avoid turning your system into a huge, hulking cow, burdened with files and consequently sluggish. You can create two batch files, DF.BAT and SIZE.BAT, to help you keep a rein on things.

DF stands for Disk Free, and DF.BAT uses the Chkdsk and Find commands to show you how space is being used on your hard disk. Figure 2-5 shows the commands in DF.BAT. Use your favorite text editor or the MS-DOS Editor to create this file, and then save it with the name DF.BAT.

Basically, this program redirects the output from the Chkdsk command to a file on disk called SIZE.IS. That file is then scanned for key text using

```
1: @echo off
2: chkdsk > size.is
3: copy size.is free.is > nul
4: find "total disk" size.is
5: find "available on" free.is
6: del *.is
```

Figure 2-5. *The DF.BAT batch file.*

the Find command. You can get the same information using Chkdsk, but
DF.BAT formats the output of Chkdsk, making it prettier and more useful.
Here is a sample run:

```
C>df
---------- SIZE.IS
  42366976 bytes total disk space

---------- FREE.IS
  20267008 bytes available on disk
```

In this example, the hard disk is more than half full; of some 40 megabytes, 20 megabytes are still available.

The SIZE.BAT program works like DF.BAT, except that SIZE reports the
number of bytes used in a single subdirectory. The script for SIZE.BAT is
shown in Figure 2-6. Use your text editor or the MS-DOS Editor to create
this file and then save it to disk as SIZE.BAT. Here is a sample run:

```
C>size
 Directory of C:\MS-DOS
       84 file(s)     2085271 bytes
                      20264960 bytes free
```

As you can see, the SIZE batch file tells you how many files are in the current directory and how many bytes they occupy. The last line tells you
how many bytes are still available on the hard disk.

You can follow SIZE with the name of a directory to examine any directory without having to first change to that directory:

```
C>size \
 Directory of C:\
       15 file(s)      117648 bytes
                      20264960 bytes free
```

In this example, 117,648 bytes are used by 15 files (and subdirectories) in
the root directory.

```
1: @echo off
2: dir %1 | find "Directory"
3: dir %1 | find "bytes"
```

Figure 2-6. *The SIZE.BAT batch file.*

Just as DF uses the output of Chkdsk, SIZE simply pares down the output of the Dir command, giving you only the name of the directory and the byte-count summary. Still, SIZE.BAT is a quick way to check a sub-directory's bloat factor: If the number of files or the size in bytes seems abnormally large, perhaps it's time to split that directory into subdirectories and move some files.

Note that the SIZE program does not report the number of bytes used by the files if you are running MS-DOS version 4.01 or earlier.

THE TAO OF MS-DOS: SELECTING THE CORRECT PATH

One advantage of being lazy and keeping all of your files in the root directory—perhaps the only advantage—is that you don't have to worry about your search path. In fact, many installation programs routinely put the root directory in the search path for precisely that (incorrect) reason.

The search path is a list of directories that MS-DOS shuffles through, looking for programs to run. Whenever you enter something at the prompt, MS-DOS first checks to see if it's an internal command (such as Copy, Dir, or Ren). If it isn't, MS-DOS looks in the current directory for a COM, EXE, or BAT file with that name. If it comes up empty, MS-DOS then checks the search path, which is a list of subdirectories stored in memory in a place called the *environment*. Each directory is checked for a COM, EXE, or BAT file whose name matches what you typed. If nothing turns up, you see the famous *Bad command or file name* error message. Then what do you do? Start over.

The search path can include any directory you want. You can use the Path or Set commands to create it. Simply list the subdirectories in which you want MS-DOS to look for files, separating directory names with semico-lons. For example:

```
C>path c:\win;c:\ms-dos;c:\util
```

This command places the WIN (Windows), MS-DOS, and UTIL sub-directories "in the path." MS-DOS will be able to find and run programs in those directories no matter which other directory or drive you're currently in. You can also use the Set command to create the same search path:

```
C>set path=c:\win;c:\ms-dos;c:\util
```

Obviously, your system's search path should reflect your own subdirectory organization, and it's usually best to create one master path in your AUTOEXEC.BAT file and then forget about it. But you pay a performance tax for a long, cumbersome path—just as you pay a penalty for an unorganized hard disk.

MS-DOS allows you to type up to 127 characters at the MS-DOS prompt, which means your path can contain up to 122 characters (127 minus 5 characters for the word *path* and a space) or about a dozen subdirectories. Depending on how clever you are, you can add many more directories to the path. That might sound great: You can access any COM, EXE, or BAT program in any of those subdirectories. Now consider this: Your cat walks across the keyboard. It spells ASXCLJK and kicks the Enter key. Thinking your cat wants to run a program, MS-DOS looks for an internal command named ASXCLJK. Then it looks for a matching COM, EXE, or BAT file in the current directory and in all the directories on the path. The result: Your computer is a listless slug. Even programs on the path take a few seconds to run because MS-DOS has to hunt for them.

A long path definitely isn't the most efficient solution. Instead, a nice trim path with perhaps two or three subdirectories is the key to running a responsive system. You can trim down your search path with batch files.

Keeping Your Search Path Short

Batch files can be complex, like the DF.BAT and SIZE.BAT programs listed earlier in this chapter. But most batch files will be simple shortcuts, primarily designed to pare down your system's search path. For example, consider this basic path:

C:\WIN;C:\M S-DOS;C:\B ATCH

Here, Windows, MS-DOS, and a special batch-file directory are located in the path. It's short and sweet. Other subdirectories need not be included in the path, providing you create batch files to run the programs contained within them.

A batch file that runs a program doesn't have to be complex; all that's needed is *@echo off*, a Cd command, and the command to start the program. For example, suppose the Q&A application is in the C:\Q&A directory. If that directory isn't in the search path, you'll need to enter two MS-DOS commands to run Q&A: *cd \q&a* and *qa*. Put those commands into a batch file, and you have

```
@echo off
cd \q&a
qa
```

Save the batch file to disk as QA.BAT, put it in your BATCH directory (which is in the path), and you'll always have access to the program.

Generally you'll create two types of batch files to run programs. The first type is basic. For example, here is a batch file to run a communications program:

```
@echo off
c:
cd \comm\pcomm
pcplus
```

It starts with the *@echo off* command. Then *c:* logs to drive C, *cd* changes to the correct subdirectory, and *pcplus* runs the program. You can create a batch file like this one for each of your programs. Or you can create the following variation:

```
@echo off
c:
cd \wp51
wp %1
```

Essentially, this second type of batch file is identical to the first type, except for the command-line variable %1 after the program name. This variable allows you to load a data file into the program just as if you had typed the filename after the program name at the MS-DOS prompt. In this particular example, if you named the batch file WDPERF.BAT, you could enter *wdperf memojohn.wp* to switch to the WP51 directory, load WordPerfect, and open the file named MEMOJOHN.WP for editing.

Placing batch files that run programs in a common BATCH or UTIL sub-directory means you can remove the corresponding program directories from your path. So it makes sense to write batch files to run programs, especially if you run only one program in a directory.

WORKING WITH FILES

When you're not organizing files into subdirectories, you'll probably be doing basic *housekeeping* chores on your hard disk. These chores involve using MS-DOS and its file manipulation commands, Copy, Ren, and Del, to move, delete, and organize your files—routine stuff. In this section, we look at two other useful commands. To help protect your data and get the most from MS-DOS while performing these chores, you can turn on the Verify command, which provides insurance that all files you copy are identical to their originals. And in addition to Copy, you can use the uncelebrated MS-DOS command Xcopy, which works like Copy but better. In fact, Xcopy is a must for hard-disk organizers.

Turning on Verify

When MS-DOS duplicates a file using the Copy command, it checks only once to ensure that the duplicate is identical to the original. Because most disks are reliable, that's about all you need; the duplicate will always match the original, and you don't need to spend the night up in bed biting your nails.

If you want MS-DOS to double-check the work of the Copy command, specify the command's /V switch. For example:

```
C>copy *.doc *.bak /v
```

Using this switch forces MS-DOS to reread every disk sector the Copy command creates. MS-DOS compares the new sector with the same sector of the original file, checking for a match. This extra protection makes file copying take longer, but you're assured that the copy is correct. For questionable disks, nothing beats it.

You can turn on the verification option for all MS-DOS disk operations by using the Verify command. For example, you could stick the following command into your AUTOEXEC.BAT file:

```
verify on
```

With verification turned on, MS-DOS double-checks all disk writes, and, as you would expect, all disk writes then take longer. To turn off verification, use this command:

```
C>verify off
```

There is no visual confirmation, though you can check the current state of the Verify command by entering *verify* by itself at the MS-DOS prompt, like this:

```
C>verify
VERIFY is off
```

Personally, I don't recommend using *verify on* unless a disk shows signs of age; the degraded performance Verify introduces just isn't worth it. (Back in the days of floppy-disk–only computing, it was.) If you want verification turned on under certain circumstances, then use the /V switch with the Copy command.

Using the Xcopy Command

The Xcopy command is like a super Copy command. It's been described as a cross between the Copy and Backup commands, but that description isn't really correct. Unlike Backup, Xcopy cannot copy files across several disks. (If you try, you'll get the *Disk full* error message.) However, this limitation doesn't detract from its value.

The fundamental rule for using Xcopy goes like this: Whenever you would normally use the Copy command, use Xcopy instead. As long as you have MS-DOS version 3.2 or later, you have Xcopy, so why not take advantage of it?

One of Xcopy's key advantages is that it copies a whole gang of files faster than Copy. The Copy command reads and writes one file at a time, which is like moving books between two bookshelves one book at a time. Xcopy reads as many files as will fit in memory and then writes them before going back to read the next batch—like stacking dozens of books on your arms and then moving them that way. For example:

```
C>xcopy *.* a:
Reading source file(s)...
```

The message *Reading source file(s)* means Xcopy is reading all the files in the current directory (*.*) into memory (or as many files as will fit). Copying them with the Xcopy command takes about a third of the time copying with the Copy command would.

Further benefits come from Xcopy's optional switches. These allow you to control which files are copied and to tell Xcopy to look in subdirectories.

Xcopy's /S and /E switches are often used together to copy files in subdirectories. The /S switch instructs Xcopy to look for matching files in all subdirectories under the source directory. Those files are copied to the destination, and if their subdirectories don't exist, Xcopy creates them. The /E switch directs Xcopy to create empty destination subdirectories as well. (The /E switch works only when you specify *.* as the source file.)

The best time to use the /S and /E switches is when you're copying an entire subdirectory branch. For example, suppose you move your WP51 directory into a general word-processing directory with this command:

```
C>xcopy c:\wp51\*.* c:\words /s/e
```

Everything in the C:\WP51 directory—files, subdirectories, and their files and subdirectories—is copied to the C:\WORDS directory. Of course, your next step is to go back to C:\WP51 and delete all the files and subdirectories. Unfortunately, Xcopy doesn't move files; it only copies them.

Xcopy has three switches that make it similar to the Backup command. They're listed in Table 2-2, along with what they do.

TABLE 2-2. XCOPY'S "BACKUP" SWITCHES

Switch	Function
/D:*date*	Copy files with a date later than *date*
/A	Copy files that have their archive attribute set but don't reset the attribute
/M	Copy files that have their archive attribute set and reset the attribute after they're copied

For example, if you want to copy files created or modified after a certain date, you can use the following command:

```
C>xcopy \project\*.* a: /d:12-14-92
```

In this example, only those files with a date later than 12-14-92 are copied to drive A.

You use the /A switch to copy files modified since the last backup—sort of an incremental backup, except that the /A switch doesn't affect a file's archive attribute (as the /M switch does). For example, the command

```
C>xcopy c:\word\projects\pamphlet\*.* a: /a
```

could be part of a daily backup routine; it copies all the modified files in the PAMPHLET directory to drive A. If you want Xcopy to ignore these files the next time you back them up, use the /M switch to turn off the files' archive attributes as they are copied.

Finally, Xcopy has two prompting switches: /P and /W. The /P switch causes Xcopy to display a *(Y/N)?* prompt after each filename; press Y to copy the file or press N to skip it. The /W switch causes Xcopy to display the message *Press any key to begin copying file(s)*. This switch comes in handy in batch files. For example:

```
@echo off
rem Create work-files backup using Xcopy
echo Insert daily work backup disk into drive A
xcopy c:\work\*.* a: /s/w
```

When you run this batch file, it displays the following messages:

```
Insert daily work backup disk into drive A
Press any key to begin copying file(s)
```

Xcopy is extremely handy, so don't let its parade of switches intimidate you. Personally, I recommend using Xcopy any time you'd normally use Copy. Beyond that, remember the /S and /E switches for copying files in subdirectories. They make Xcopy a powerful ally for anyone who needs to organize their hard disk.

ARCHIVING FILES

Archiving files means storing them for later use—usually storing them somewhere other than on the hard disk. Archiving could imply backing up, though backup procedures are really for file security and safety. Usually, archiving is simply copying files to floppies for storage, or compressing and compacting files on the hard disk to keep them handy but manageable.

Archiving to Floppies

I hate to sound prehistoric, but in the old days we kept everything on floppy disks in a handsome $19.95 disk caddy (which had more prestige if it had the name and logo of your computer company on it). That disk caddy is still useful. It's great for storing disks with old project files, graphics files, libraries, and other data you don't need on your hard disk. In fact, brushing that stuff off onto floppies often cleans up megabytes of hard-disk space.

What you archive is up to you. If it all fits on one floppy disk—great. Archiving is an ideal opportunity for the Xcopy command to show its stuff. For example, to archive some old Windows bitmap files (*.BMP) on a floppy disk, you can use the following command:

```
C>xcopy \win\*.bmp a: /s
```

All the bitmap (*.BMP) files are copied from the WIN directory and all its subdirectories to the floppy disk in drive A. Label the disk properly and stow it away. Delete the originals from the hard disk, and you have more space in which to play.

If the files don't easily fit onto a single disk, you can use the Backup command to archive them. In addition to performing the basic boring backup chore, MS-DOS's Backup program can also copy large files across several floppy disks. I store mega graphics images and old desktop-publishing files on floppy disks all the time. For example, I can use the command

```
C>backup \dtp\*.gra a: /s
```

to copy all the *.GRA (graphics) files from my DTP directory and all its subdirectories to the disk in drive A. If more than one disk is needed,

Backup prompts me to insert them. After that's done, I label the disks, bundle them with a rubber band, and put them into my very own Microsoft disk caddy.

If your system is connected to a network server, you should consider archiving your files on the server. Check with your network administrator first. You might find that you have a few megabytes of your own "space" on the server, in which case you can use it to store files you don't immediately need. (And the cool part about that is that the network administrator backs up the server; you don't have to worry about it.) If the files would benefit other users, consider plopping them down in a public directory instead.

Compressing Files

To most PC users, "archiving" implies packing many small files into one large file. Thanks to complex mathematical compression algorithms, that one large file actually takes up less space than all the smaller files. This magic allows you to store many related files in one compact file—and still keep everything handy on your hard disk.

I routinely pack all chapter files, graphics images, outlines, programs, figures, and tables from my books into one handy archive file after the book is completed. That way, using the PKZIP archiving program, text from an entire book sits in a single file that occupies far less disk space.

Many programs for compacting and storing files are on the market. My favorite is PKZIP from PKWare, Inc., in Wisconsin. It allows you to compress many files—even across subdirectories—into one handy "zip" file. Files can be extracted one at a time or all at once using the PKUNZIP program, and other utility programs (such as Lotus' Magellan) allow you to examine the contents of a zip file to see what's inside. Using PKZIP is a handy way of storing information without that information gobbling up disk space.

You can pick up PKZIP and PKUNZIP from a users' group, a national on-line system, a software clearing house, or from PKWare itself. For a software clearing house, I recommend PC-SIG. In the United States, you can call them at 1-800-245-6717 and ask for Disk 1364. If you want to order directly from PKWare, the address is PKWARE, Inc., 7545 N. Port Washington Rd., Glendale, WI 53217.

SUMMARY

Keeping your house in order means working with files on your hard disk. That job is done much more easily if you have a well-organized system of subdirectories into which you place related files.

The next chapter continues the theme of performance boosting by concentrating on MS-DOS commands and how to make them work smarter.

Chapter 3

Building MS-DOS Muscle

MS-DOS does a reliable job of managing files and disks, but it's not perfect. With only a few simple modifications—primarily using *smart batch files*—you can add muscle to MS-DOS. This can be really fun, and it's the way most inventors make a living: Take a job everyone does every day and figure out a way to do it more conveniently.

This chapter is about squeezing more power out of MS-DOS—by inventing batch files that make the everyday things you do with MS-DOS easier and safer. The first part of this chapter shows several ingenious batch files that take the risk out of using MS-DOS's file-manipulation commands. The second part discusses ways to patch up MS-DOS—actually removing and replacing MS-DOS commands. The third part of the chapter deals with managing floppy disks, and gives you a killer batch file for formatting floppies.

SMART BATCH FILES

You should use batch files to run most applications on your PC. Simply plop the batch files into a common BATCH directory and put that directory in your path. Nothing could be easier.

Batch files can also handle common chores: backing up files, setting up external devices, intializing printers, or any of a number of repetitive MS-DOS tasks. Batch files can carry out an amazing number of tasks. The most useful batch files are smart ones that replace some rather unintelligent (and dangerous) MS-DOS commands.

The following sections contain batch file replacements for the Copy and Del commands, plus an interesting Move command. Create each of these handy batch files and place them in your BATCH or UTIL subdirectories. To make them useful, put that directory first in your system's search path. For example:

```
path c:\batch;c:\ms-dos;c:\win
```

Modify the Path command in your AUTOEXEC.BAT file accordingly, so you'll always have access to these smart batch files.

A Safer Way to Copy Files

The Copy command never tells you if a file that has the same name as the file you're copying already exists on the "target" drive or subdirectory. If a file with the same name exists, it is overwritten by the copied file. When this happens, not even the best data-recovery program can get the original file back. Wouldn't it be swell if MS-DOS warned you when the Copy command was about to overwrite a file?

Consider the CP.BAT batch file shown in Figure 3-1.

```
 1: @echo off
 2: rem cp, a better copy program
 3: rem copy files from %1 to %2
 4:
 5: rem test parameters
 6: if %1!==! goto WARNING
 7: if %2!==! goto WARNING
 8:
 9: rem test for existence of duplicate files
10: if not exist %2 goto CP01
11: echo %2 already exists!
12: goto END
13:
14: :CP01
15: rem test for subdirectory\file(s)
16: if not exist %2\%1 goto CP02
17: echo %2\%1 already exists!
18: goto END
19:
20: :CP02
21: rem test for drive:file(s)
22: if not exist %2%1 goto CP03
23: echo %2%1 already exists!
24: goto END
25:
26: :CP03
27: echo Copying file(s)...
28: copy %1 %2 >nul
29: echo Files copied
30: goto END
31:
32: :WARNING
33: echo CP format: cp source destination
34:
35: :END
```

Figure 3-1. *CP.BAT provides a better Copy command.*

CP.BAT provides the Copy command plus safety checking. It looks ahead to see if the target file already exists—under three different circumstances. If the file exists, a warning appears and the target file is preserved. Yeah!

Create CP.BAT using your favorite text editor or the MS-DOS Editor. Save it in your BATCH directory as CP.BAT. Use the CP command instead of the Copy command when you do not want files to be overwritten. For example:

```
C>cp vital.doc a:
Copying file(s)...
Files copied
```

If VITAL.DOC already existed on drive A, you'd see the following:

```
C>cp vital.doc a:
a:\vital.doc already exists!
```

Here's a line-by-line description of what CP.BAT does.

Line 1 turns off the echo. Lines 2 and 3 contain remarks about the CP program. Line 4 is blank, as are lines 8, 13, 19, 25, 31, and 34. Blank lines are entirely legal in a batch file, and they help make the listing easier to read and understand, especially in long batch files.

Line 5 describes lines 6 and 7, which test for CP's two required parameters, %1 and %2. If either parameter is missing, execution branches to the *WARNING* label at line 32.

Line 9 describes lines 10 through 12, which test for an existing target file using a simple If Not Exist test in line 10. If the target file doesn't exist, execution branches to the *CP01* label in line 14; otherwise, the message *%2 already exists!* is displayed and execution branches to the *END* label at line 35. (MS-DOS replaces %2 in the message with the name of the matching file.)

Lines 14 through 18 perform a second test, this time for cases when the target is a subdirectory instead of a filename. MS-DOS tests for the file's existence using an If Not Exist statement in line 16. If the target file %1 doesn't exist in the subdirectory %2, execution branches to the *CP02* label at line 20; otherwise, the message *%2\%1 already exists!* is displayed.

MS-DOS replaces *%2* with the subdirectory name and *%1* with the file-name, and execution branches to the *END* label at line 35.

Lines 20 through 24 perform a third test, for cases when you copy to a drive letter only. Line 22 uses an If Not Exist test for the drive letter, for *%2*, and for the filename, *%1*. If the target file doesn't exist on that drive, execution branches to the *CP03* label at line 26. If the file does exist, the message *%2%1 already exists!* is displayed and execution then branches to the *END* label at line 35.

After all tests are complete, lines 26 through 30 copy the designated file. The standard Copy command is used in line 28, with its output redirected to the NUL device.

This batch file isn't foolproof. It tests for only three conditions under which a file exists. If you specify a wildcard, the CP command assumes *any* match to be deadly, and it doesn't copy a single file. (In a way, that's a blessing.)

With modification, CP.BAT could do more extensive checking, but that checking would slow down the batch file. As listed, CP.BAT provides a quick, safe alternative to the Copy command.

A Smarter Way to Delete Files

The Del (or Erase) command can be deadly. Even with something like the Mirror program's Deletion Tracking (see Chapter 6) and the Undelete command, you should never be negligent or sloppy when deleting files. A better solution is simply to not delete files, but instead "put them away" and delete them later, when they're no longer needed. Although putting files away doesn't free up any disk space, it does save you from the pains of undeleting files, and it virtually guarantees that any files you put away can be recovered easily.

I call this system the *Trash Can method* of deleting files, borrowing the term from another type of personal computer. Instead of deleting files, you use a special command to place the files in a "trash-can" directory. It's al-most as though the files are deleted; they're out of sight but not really gone—as if they're in a can on the curb waiting for collection.

Later, you can browse through the trash-can directory and delete files you know you don't need, pluck out those you still want, or run a special "empty trash" command to delete the files. As you can probably guess, you can do all of this with batch files.

Start by creating the trash-can directory. I call mine TRASH, and it branches off the root directory of drive C:

```
C>md \trash
```

No one likes to look at trash, so make the TRASH directory invisible by using the Attrib command:

```
C>attrib +h \trash
```

Note: It's possible to hide the directory using a special batch file such as HIDE.BAT, which is presented in Chapter 6.

After the trash can is created and hidden from view, you need two special batch files: one to toss things into the trash and another to empty the trash. The first program is called TRASH.BAT, and it's shown in Figure 3-2.

Create TRASH.BAT using your text editor or the MS-DOS Editor. Save the file in your BATCH directory as TRASH.BAT.

TRASH.BAT is basically a file-moving batch file: It takes files from one location, copies them to the TRASH directory, and then deletes the original files. To run the TRASH.BAT program, enter *trash* followed by the names of one or more files. For example:

```
C>trash readme.doc
readme.doc moved to trash
```

The file README.DOC moves to the trash; it is effectively gone.

```
1: @echo off
2: :START
3: if %1!==! goto END
4: copy %1 c:\trash >nul
5: echo y | del %1 >nul
6: echo %1 moved to trash
7: shift
8: goto START
9: :END
```

Figure 3-2. *The TRASH.BAT program deletes files.*

Because TRASH.BAT contains a loop, you can move multiple files to the
trash by specifying more than one filename at the MS-DOS prompt:

```
C>trash oldfile.doc *.bak payroll.wk2
oldfile.doc moved to trash
*.bak moved to trash
payroll.wk2 moved to trash
```

The TRASH.BAT program uses line 3 to determine if you specified a
filename. If not, the program ends (at line 9). Otherwise, the file is copied
to the trash-can directory (in line 4), and the original file is deleted (in line
5). The message *%1 moved to trash* is echoed in line 6, and the command-
line variables are shifted (in line 7). Then the program loops back to line 2
to check for additional files to copy to the trash.

Batch-file whizzes should take note of line 5. If the *.* wildcard is used,
the Del command responds with a warning and a yes/no prompt. If this
occurs, the Echo command enters *Y* and a carriage return (Enter key)
using the pipe symbol (|). This trick supplies input to MS-DOS commands
much better than input redirection, which requires a text file with the
proper keystrokes elsewhere on disk. (This subject is covered in detail in
Supercharging MS-DOS, published by Microsoft Press.)

The only problem with trashing files instead of using the Del command is
that it doesn't free up any disk space. To free up disk space, you must
empty the trash-can directory. This can be done with the EMPTY.BAT program shown in Figure 3-3.

Create this file using your text editor or the MS-DOS Editor. Save the file
in your BATCH directory as EMPTY.BAT.

The EMPTY.BAT program needs only line 4, which uses the Del command
to delete all the files in the TRASH directory. As with TRASH.BAT, the
Echo command and a pipe symbol are used to supply a Y and a carriage
return to the Del *.* command's *Are you sure?* prompt.

```
1: @echo off
2: ask Empty the trash?
3: if errorlevel 1 goto END
4: echo y | del c:\trash\*.* >nul
5: echo Trash is empty
6: :END
```

Figure 3-3. *The EMPTY.BAT program empties the trash-can directory.*

But instead of simply deleting the files in the trash, EMPTY.BAT plays it safe: Line 2 uses the Ask command to prompt you, asking if you're sure you want to empty the trash. If you press Y, the Ask command returns an errorlevel of 0. Otherwise, it returns a value of 1, and execution branches to the *END* label at line 6.

Here is a sample run of the EMPTY.BAT program:

```
C>empty
Empty the trash? Y
Trash is empty
```

This program frees up the disk space used by the files in the TRASH directory. I recommend that you look over the files before using the Empty command, so you can rescue any gems you might have inadvertently "trashed." Another problem with the Trash and Empty commands is teaching them to other users: Remember to tell other users to "trash" files, not Del or Erase them. You might want to consider the following:

```
C>copy \batch\trash.bat \batch\kill.bat
```

This creates a duplicate of the TRASH.BAT file named KILL.BAT. Some users might remember to "kill" a file rather than "trash" a file. (And *kill* is easier to spell for most people.)

Another potential problem is that you might not have the ASK program. If you don't, use the Debug script in Figure 3-4 to create it. Simply type those commands into a text file named ASK.SCR. Double-check your work. Then enter the following MS-DOS command:

```
C>debug <ask.scr
```

```
n ask.com
e100 A0 80 00 3C 00 74 26 98
e108 8B C8 BB 82 00 E8 33 00
e110 B4 08 CD 21 24 5F 3C 59
e118 74 0E 3C 4E 75 F2 8A D0
e120 E8 0F 00 B8 01 4C CD 21
e128 8A D0 E8 05 00 B8 00 4C
e130 CD 21 B4 02 CD 21 B2 0D
e138 B4 02 CD 21 B2 0A B4 02
e140 CD 21 C3 8A 17 80 FA 0D
e148 74 07 B4 02 CD 21 43 E2
e150 F2 B2 20 B4 02 CD 21 C3
rcx
58
w
q
```

Figure 3-4. *The ASK.COM script file, ASK.SCR.*

The ASK.COM program will be created. Copy it to your UTILITY, BATCH, or other subdirectory listed in the path, so your batch files will always have access to it. (Do the same for the other programs in this chapter created with Debug.)

ASK.COM waits for you to press either Y or N. If you press Y, the program returns an errorlevel of 0; if you press N, it returns a value of 1. You can use ASK.COM in batch files to help you make decisions or to warn you of impending doom.

A More Efficient Way to Move Files

Another handy file utility is a Move program. Like TRASH.BAT (described in the previous section), this program copies a file and then deletes the original.

The MOVE.BAT program shown in Figure 3-5 duplicates files using the Copy command. The Del command then deletes the original files. Create MOVE.BAT using your text editor or the MS-DOS Editor. Save the file in your batch-file directory as MOVE.BAT.

Lines 3 and 4 ensure that all the parameters have been entered. The Move program requires both a source and a target file—just like the Copy command. If either the source or target file is missing, execution branches to the *WARNING* label at line 12.

Line 6 echoes the *Moving files* message. The files are copied (in line 7) and the originals are deleted (in line 8). Note how the Echo command is used to supply input for any warning prompt Del might display.

```
 1: @echo off
 2: rem this moves files from %1 to %2
 3: if %1!==! goto WARNING
 4: if %2!==! goto WARNING
 5:
 6: echo Moving files...
 7: copy %1 %2 >nul
 8: echo y | del %1 >nul
 9: echo Files moved
10: goto END
11:
12: :WARNING
13: echo Move format: move source destination
14: :END
```

Figure 3-5. *The MOVE.BAT program moves files (copies and deletes).*

Line 9 displays the *Files moved* message, indicating that the move operation is complete. Execution then branches to the *END* label at line 14.

Using the Move program is a fairly simple operation:

```
C>move *.dbf a:
Moving files...
Files moved
```

Always remember that the original files are deleted. Of course, you can combine MOVE.BAT with other batch files. For example, consider changing line 8 in MOVE.BAT to read

```
call trash %1
```

This "trashes" the moved files, which is safer than deleting them outright.

PATCHING MS-DOS

One way to make MS-DOS smarter is to perform *brain surgery*—on the computer, not on yourself! With computer programs, this brain surgery is referred to as *patching*, or the art of modifying an existing program using special patching tools such as the MS-DOS Debug utility. By patching, you can make programs perform better and sometimes eliminate some of the sillier things they do.

As with brain surgery, changing any program is a delicate and potentially dangerous thing to do. I don't recommend patching MS-DOS as a passing fancy; it's not worth the risk. But in some instances, modifying MS-DOS programs can be beneficial.

Putting the Beep Back into Backup

In versions of MS-DOS earlier than version 5, the Backup utility always beeped to prompt you to insert a backup disk. With MS-DOS 5, however, the Backup program stopped beeping. If you didn't like or don't miss the beep, you're thankful. If you miss the beep, you can patch Backup to reinstate the beep.

Putting a beep into Backup works by placing a Ctrl-G character into the text string *Press any key to continue.* (Ctrl-G, or ASCII 7, is the "character" that causes the PC's speaker to beep.) Because Backup displays *Press any key to continue* before it asks for a disk, this is how you can sound the beep.

The Backup program is named BACKUP.EXE. To patch it, you must use the Debug utility. However, Debug works best with COM or BIN files; loading an EXE file such as Backup can yield unpredictable results. To patch an EXE file, you must rename it as a BIN (binary) file. Before doing that, make a backup copy of the original file. In your MS-DOS directory, enter the following at the prompt:

```
C>copy backup.exe backup.bak
      1 file(s) copied
```

Now you can rename the original as a BIN file:

```
C>ren backup.exe backup.bin
```

After you have renamed BACKUP.EXE as BACKUP.BIN, you can use Debug to patch it. Load the Backup program into Debug with the following command:

```
C>debug backup.bin
-
```

Debug loads Backup and then shows its prompt, the hyphen (-). To search for the text string *Press any key to continue*, use the S (Search) command. This is the S command's syntax:

   S *start end "string"*

Start is the starting location, always 100 hexadecimal. The *end* value is the ending location, or the length of the file if it's preceded by an *L*. Using FFFF for the end value works in all cases. Enter the following Debug command:

```
-s 100 ffff "Press any key to continue"
xxxx:4FE3
```

Debug returns the address, or memory location, of that string in memory. The first four numbers, designated above as *xxxx*, vary from computer to computer. The second four numbers are important. In the example, 4FE3, the location of the string, is returned. Using that value, or whatever value appeared on your screen, enter the following command:

```
-d 4fe3
```

Press Enter and you'll see the string of text in memory. It will be in a three-column format, as shown in Figure 3-6. The first column shows memory locations, the second shows byte values at those locations, and the third column shows ASCII characters.

In Figure 3-6, you can see the string *Press any key to continue* in the rightmost column. The string ends with a carriage-return/line-feed combination, shown by the byte characters 0D and 0A in row 5000. If you take the final period in the screen, the 2E character at row 5000, second column, and change it to the Ctrl-G character, the beep will be "displayed," or sounded.

To change the 2E, a period, to 07, the Ctrl-G character, use the E command. The 2E is at memory location 5001 (row 5000, column 1; columns are numbered starting with 0 in Debug). Here is the E command:

```
-e 5001 07
```

Note: To remove a beep, you would replace a 07 character with a 20 character—a space.

Remember to specify the proper location: Look for the final period in the string. It should be a 2E character, as seen in the middle column. Use that character's row number, and then count over to it starting with 0. Debug uses the hexadecimal counting system, so the values 10 through 15 are read as A through F.

Verify that the period has been changed; retype the original D command to display memory:

```
-d 4fe3
```

Be sure the four-digit value is proper for your system. Then confirm that the 2E was properly replaced with a 07 character. If not, quit Debug by entering *Q*, and then start the whole procedure over again.

```
-d4fe3
1E1B:4FE0                   50 72 65 73 73-20 61 6E 79 20 6B 65 79      Press any key
1E1B:4FF0   20 74 6F 20 63 6F 6E 74-69 6E 75 65 20 2E 20 2E   to continue . .
1E1B:5000   20 2E 0D 0A 02 0D 0A 28-0D 0A 43 61 6E 6E 6F 74    ......(..Cannot
1E1B:5010   20 46 4F 52 4D 41 54 20-6E 6F 6E 72 65 6D 6F 76    FORMAT nonremov
1E1B:5020   61 62 6C 65 20 64 72 69-76 65 20 25 31 3A 0D 0A   able drive %1:..
1E1B:5030   71 0D 0A 42 65 63 61 75-73 65 20 79 6F 75 72 20   q..Because your
1E1B:5040   73 6F 75 72 63 65 20 64-72 69 76 65 20 69 73 20   source drive is
1E1B:5050   65 69 74 68 65 72 20 41-53 53 49 47 4E 65 64 2C   either ASSIGNed,
1E1B:5060   20 4A 4F                                          JO
```

Figure 3-6. *Debug finds the string to patch in memory.*

If the 07 character sits in the proper position, save BACKUP.BIN using the W command:

```
-W
```

Debug responds by displaying the number of bytes written to disk (in hexa-decimal). Quit Debug by entering *Q*.

Back at the MS-DOS prompt, rename BACKUP.BIN to its original name:

```
C>ren backup.bin backup.exe
```

You're now ready to test the program and listen for the beep. Try backing up just a few files with the following command:

```
C>backup c:\*.* a:
```

This will back up only the files in the root directory, which should be few if you're following this book closely. Press Enter:

```
Insert backup diskette 01 in drive B:

WARNING! Files in the target drive
B:\ root directory will be erased
Press any key to continue..
```

If everything worked, the message will display only two periods, and the computer will beep! Backup has been patched; feel free to delete BACKUP.BAK, the safety copy.

If patching didn't work, nothing will happen. Patching a file with a single Ctrl-G character is relatively minor, so if you don't hear a beep when you run Backup, press Ctrl-C to cancel the program. Then delete the BACKUP.EXE file and recover the original file by entering *ren backup.bak backup.exe*.

Although patching a program to add—or remove—a beep is relatively minor, knowing that you can improve upon MS-DOS can make you a little power-crazy. Other patches are possible as well, but you should always have a clear purpose in mind before attempting any patch.

Patching COMMAND.COM

Patching external MS-DOS commands is a moderately complex process done by using Debug to alter their internal functions. Changing text strings, as demonstrated in the previous section, is relatively easy. Changing programming code requires skill and a knowledge of MS-DOS programming. Yet patching can sometimes be as simple as renaming a command.

For example, you can rename FORMAT.COM as DISKPREP.COM. Then you can write a FORMAT.BAT file—which calls the DISKPREP.COM file internally—to format disks and safeguard against accidental reformatting.

Beyond external MS-DOS commands lie the important internal commands. The internal commands are more exacting to modify because they're held in the center of the command processor, COMMAND.COM. Sound the warning trumpets!

Patching the command processor is a scary thing. The only real reason to patch COMMAND.COM is to rename the internal MS-DOS commands and replace them with like-named batch files. For example, you could patch the MS-DOS Copy command, renaming it Xxyx inside COMMAND.COM. Then you could rename the CP.BAT file COPY.BAT, rename the Copy command inside COPY.BAT Xxyx, and you'd have a truly better Copy command.

The tricky part is that you must be exact: You must find the precise command you are modifying, very carefully replace it, and then test COMMAND.COM to be sure it works. Obviously, this isn't for the casual MS-DOS user.

To patch COMMAND.COM's internal commands, you must locate its command list, the section of the program that lists all MS-DOS commands in a special format. The actual MS-DOS command names appear all over the place inside COMMAND.COM—especially with MS-DOS 5's help messages in the same file. But you can locate the list.

The following steps in Debug *will not* change COMMAND.COM. If you want to do so, you're on your own. Remember to make a backup copy.

Load COMMAND.COM into Debug with the following command:

```
C>debug command.com
```

Search for an MS-DOS command, such as COPY, using the S (Search) command within Debug:

```
-s 100 ffff "COPY"
1E37:89BA
1E37:A93B
1E37:C4CB
```

You must type *COPY* in uppercase letters. A few matches will appear on your screen, as shown above. Odds are pretty good that the last match is the command name itself. Use the D (Display) command to display that area of memory. For example:

```
-d c4cb
```

You'll see the word *COPY* displayed at the right side of the screen. If you see parts of the syntax line for the Copy command, you've got the help information. Try displaying one of the other locations that the S command listed. If you see COPY and other MS-DOS commands as well, such as PAUSE, DATE, TIME, and VER, you've found the internal command list. Use the E command to patch the MS-DOS command text; replace it with your own command text—in uppercase letters. The new command name must be exactly the same length as the original command name.

If you make modifications, enter W to write the patched command interpreter back to disk. Otherwise, enter Q to exit Debug. If you haven't made any changes, everything will work as before. Personally, I don't recommend patching COMMAND.COM; writing clever batch files is a better alternative.

Note: If you do patch COMMAND.COM, rename it first. For example, copy COMMAND.COM and rename it something like TEST.COM. Run the new command processor (TEST.COM) as a shell, just as you would COMMAND.COM: Enter test *(or whatever) at the MS-DOS prompt. Experiment with the patched command interpreter, and try out your patched MS-DOS commands. If they run, fine. If not, try again. In any case, reset your PC after testing. If you decide to use the patched command interpreter, rename it COMMAND.COM again and copy it to the correct locations on your hard disk. Reset your computer to load the new command interpreter.*

A Saner Alternative: Using Doskey's Macros

Instead of patching the command processor, you can use the keyboard macro program Doskey to eliminate or replace certain MS-DOS commands. It might not be elegant, but it's definitely safer than patching COMMAND.COM.

To take advantage of Doskey, it must be loaded into memory. This is generally done using the AUTOEXEC.BAT file so that Doskey is available as soon as you start using MS-DOS. A line in AUTOEXEC.BAT such as the following will do the trick:

```
doskey /insert
```

In this example, the Doskey program is loaded into memory in the *insert* mode. Command-line editing, MS-DOS command history, and keyboard macros are available when Doskey is in memory.

To create a Doskey macro, use a format similar to the Set command:

doskey *macro=keystrokes*

Macro is the name of the macro. It can be anything—even internal MS-DOS commands, which is how you're able to patch MS-DOS using Doskey. The macro's name is followed by an equal sign, followed by the *keystrokes* or MS-DOS command which is being assigned, or "aliased." If the keystrokes contain any forbidden MS-DOS characters, they must be entered using the dollar-sign characters shown in Table 3-1.

TABLE 3-1. DOSKEY'S DOLLAR-SIGN COMMAND CHARACTERS

Macro Command	Character
$B or $b	I, pipe
$G or $g	>, greater than
$L or $l	<, less than
$T or $t	Ctrl-T (¶), command separator
$$	$, dollar sign
$1 through $9	First through ninth command-line parameters
$*	All command-line parameters

Consider the following Doskey macro:

```
C>doskey del=kill $1
```

Doskey creates the *del* macro. It's assigned to the Kill command, KILL.BAT. The $1 is the first command-line parameter, in this case, the filename or wildcard typed after the Del command.

When you enter *del* at the MS-DOS prompt, Doskey will run the Del macro instead of the Del command. The Del macro runs the KILL.BAT file, and the $1 command-line parameter passes along the name or wildcard of the file or files to delete.

Other MS-DOS commands can be aliased in this manner: Copy can be aliased to Xcopy or the CP.BAT program, Format can be aliased to the FORMAT.BAT program, and so on. You can create these in AUTOEXEC.BAT after you initially load Doskey:

```
doskey /insert
doskey del=kill $1
doskey copy=xcopy $*
doskey format=c:\batch\format.bat
```

In this example, Doskey is installed and then three macros are created. The *copy* macro is aliased to the Xcopy command, along with all the options that would follow it, as specified by the $* command character. The *format* macro is aliased to a FORMAT.BAT batch file—but with no options. It's assumed that FORMAT.BAT will ask questions about the disk to be formatted or will simply format a disk in drive A.

The one drawback is that a Doskey macro works only when it's the first element in the command line. If you type a space or a tab before the macro, the real MS-DOS command will be run instead of the macro. (Of course, this is also a handy way to get back to the original MS-DOS command when you need to.)

For a full discussion of Doskey and how it can be used, see Microsoft Press' *Supercharging MS-DOS*.

MANAGING FLOPPY DISKS

Although most computers now have hard-disk drives, the floppy disk is still handy and is used for these four general purposes:

- Backing up
- Distributing files and programs
- Transporting data
- Archiving

Whatever you use floppy disks for, properly labeling your disks is the most important aspect of managing them. I also use rubber bands to bundle related disks, backup sets, and so on.

Your main work with floppy disks is formatting them. This presents two interesting issues: formatting already-formatted disks and working with disks of various sizes and capacities. Using a few handy batch files, you can make these situations more manageable, and by using Debug to create some useful utilities, you'll discover some really ingenious ways to work with disks.

Formatting Lower-Capacity Disks

The Format command always formats a disk to the maximum capacity of the drive holding that disk. If you have a high-capacity 5¼-inch or 3½-inch drive, MS-DOS will always format a 1.2-MB or 1.4-MB (or 2.8-MB) disk in that drive. It's only when you want to format a disk of a lower capacity that you need to give Format some extra help.

Formatting low-capacity disks is necessary only when you must exchange data with a computer that has a lower-capacity drive. If you never need to do that, then you'll never need to format lower-capacity disks—or even buy them. However, if you're going to format low-capacity disks, buy that type of disk and format it to the lower capacity. Never try to format high-capacity disks as low-capacity disks. Nor should you format low-capacity disks for high capacity. I'll explain why later.

To format a low-capacity 5¼-inch disk in a high-capacity drive, use this command:

```
C>format a: /f:360
```

The /F switch followed by 360 means "Format the disk to 360 KB." (If you have MS-DOS 3.3 or earlier, use the /4 switch instead of /F.)

To format a low-capacity 3½-inch disk, use this command:

```
C>format a: /f:720
```

The /F switch followed by 720 directs the Format command to create a 720-KB disk. (If you have MS-DOS 3.3 or earlier, use the /N:9 and /T:80 switches instead of /F.) If the drive is a 2.8-MB drive and you want to format a 1.4-MB disk in it, use /F:1440 instead of /F:720.

Of course, formatting is easier if you simply write some custom batch files for your system. For example, a batch file named LOWA.BAT or AFORMAT.BAT could format a low-capacity disk in drive A, and LOWB.BAT or BFORMAT.BAT could format a low-capacity disk in drive B. These batch files can be quite simple:

```
@echo off
echo Format a low-capacity disk in drive A
format a: /f:360
```

This batch file formats a low-capacity, 360-KB 5¼-inch disk in drive A. If drive A is a 3½-inch floppy-disk drive, then you should substitute /F:720 for /F:360. You can create a similar batch file to format a low-capacity disk in drive B:

```
@echo off
echo Format a low-capacity disk in drive B
format b: /f:720
```

Again, make the proper adjustments for your B drive, specifying /F:360 or /F.720 depending on the size and capacity of the drive. Save each batch file using a name you'll remember, such as LOWA.BAT, AFORMAT.BAT, or 360.BAT.

A general batch-file solution is the LOW.BAT program, as shown in Figure 3-7. Enter this batch file using your favorite text editor or the MS-DOS Editor. Save it in your batch-file directory as LOW.BAT.

```
 1: @echo off
 2: echo Formatting a low-capacity disk
 3: getdrive
 4: if errorlevel 1 goto BFORMAT
 5: rem format low-capacity disk in A
 6: format a: /f:360
 7: goto END
 8: :BFORMAT
 9: rem format low-capacity disk in B
10: format b: /f:720
11: :END
```

Figure 3-7. *The LOW.BAT batch file formats low-capacity disks.*

LOW.BAT contains two commands to format a low-capacity disk. The first (for drive A) is located in line 6; the second (for drive B) is in line 10. Note that the commands in Figure 3-7 assume that drive A is a 5¼-inch drive and B is a 3½-inch drive. Swap the commands if your drives are arranged differently.

The key to LOW.BAT is the Getdrive command in line 3. It works similar to the Ask command shown earlier in this chapter. The difference is that Getdrive asks *Which drive (A/B)?* and waits for you to press either A or B. (The Ask command waits for a Y or N response.) If drive A is selected, Getdrive returns an errorlevel of 0; drive B returns an errorlevel of 1.

The results of the Getdrive command are evaluated in line 4 using an If Errorlevel test. The proper Format command is then carried out based on the results of the test.

To create Getdrive, enter the GETDRIVE.SCR script file, as shown in Figure 3-8. Using your text editor or the MS-DOS Editor, carefully type each line shown in Figure 3-8. Double-check your work and then save the file as GETDRIVE.SCR.

```
n getdrive.com
e100 BA 29 01 B4 09 CD 21 B4
e108 08 CD 21 24 5F 3C 41 74
e110 04 3C 42 75 F2 8A D0 B4
e118 02 CD 21 B2 0D CD 21 B2
e120 0A CD 21 2C 41 B4 4C CD
e128 21
e129 "Which drive (A/B)?$"
rcx
3c
w
q
```

Figure 3-8. *The GETDRIVE.SCR Debug script.*

Feed the GETDRIVE.SCR script file to the MS-DOS Debug utility using the following MS-DOS command:

```
C>debug <getdrive.scr
```

Debug will eat all the special codes and spit out the GETDRIVE.COM program, which you can then use in LOW.BAT or in any batch file where you want to ask the "which drive" question.

If GETDRIVE.COM doesn't work, go back and compare your script file to Figure 3-8. Correct any mistakes and then save the file again. Retry the *debug <getdrive.scr* command and everything should work fine.

Dealing with Unreadable Disks

Problems with formatting disks come in two forms: defective disks and disks formatted to the wrong capacity. You can identify a defective disk when the Format program reports a few bad sectors; toss out the disk and try again with a new one. Any other errors that occur happen when you format a disk to the wrong capacity.

The first rule of formatting is always to select the proper disk for the job: Format high-capacity disks to a high capacity; format low-capacity disks to a low capacity.

The most common problem is: You've formatted a high-capacity disk to low capacity and now you're trying to reformat it back to high capacity. You typically see the *Invalid media* or *Track 0 bad - disk unusable* error message. This means that the disk is of the wrong type and cannot be formatted to the capacity you've specified.

A quick solution is to retry the same format command, this time adding the /U switch:

```
C>format a: /u
```

The /U switch unconditionally formats the disk to the specified capacity. (Before retyping the Format command with the /U switch, you might want to double-check that the disk is of the proper capacity.)

If this doesn't work, you can try erasing the disk using a heavy-duty videotape eraser—you can pick one up at any electronics store. Energizing the magnetic particles on a disk somehow "wakes it up," and you can then format it as you like.

And if all that doesn't work, toss out the disk; it is truly unusable.

The Ultimate FORMAT.BAT Program

One of the problems with the Format command is that it never tells you that a disk is already formatted. If a disk is formatted, the Format command will save special information about the disk, allowing you to use the Unformat command later if necessary. However, that's a needless step: If the Format command blurted out *That disk's already formatted! Continue (Y/N)?*, it would save a lot of time.

Ta-da! Batch files to the rescue again. Figure 3-9 contains the ultimate disk-formatting batch file, asking all the questions the Format command

```
 1: @echo off
 2: if not %1!==! goto START
 3: echo Specify a drive letter to format.
 4: goto END
 5:
 6: :START
 7: diskin %1
 8: if errorlevel 2 goto MISSING
 9: if errorlevel 1 goto UNFORMAT
10:
11: rem disk is formatted
12: echo That disk is formatted!
13: ask Continue?
14: rem Y=0; N=1
15: if errorlevel 0 if not errorlevel 1 goto FORMAT
16: ask Format another disk?
17: if errorlevel 1 goto END
18: echo Insert disk and
19: pause
20: goto START
21:
22: :MISSING
23: echo There is no disk in that drive!
24: echo Put a disk into drive %1 and
25: pause
26: goto START
27:
28: :UNFORMAT
29: echo Unformatted disk detected
30: :FORMAT
31: echo Formatting disk...
32: c:\dos\format %1 %2 %3 /v:none <c:\batch\entern
33: cls
34: echo Format successful!
35: ask Format another disk?
36: if errorlevel 1 goto END
37: echo Remove the disk from drive A and
38: echo replace it with a new disk.
39: pause
40: goto START
41:
42: :END
```

Figure 3-9. *The ultimate batch-file Format program.*

should ask in the first place. Create the batch file using your favorite text editor or the MS-DOS Editor.

Note: Change line 32 to indicate the proper location of the MS-DOS Format program on your hard disk. If you have MS-DOS 3.3 or earlier, omit the /V:NONE switch.

When you've finished editing, save the file to your batch-file directory as FORMAT.BAT.

The file ENTERN (line 32) is simply a text file that contains Enter (a carriage return) and an N plus another carriage return. Create this file by using the following MS-DOS command:

```
C>copy con c:\batch\entern
<Enter>
n<Enter>
^Z
```

Press Ctrl-Z or F6 to end the file; ^Z will appear on your screen. Create the ENTERN file in your system's batch-file subdirectory and then be sure to put the proper pathname in line 32 of the FORMAT.BAT file.

In addition to the ENTERN file, this ultimate batch file relies on two other non–MS-DOS utilities: The Ask program (in lines 13, 16, and 35), plus the Diskin program (line 7). You learned about Ask earlier in this chapter, in Figure 3-4; it prompts you for a Y or N response and then returns an errorlevel of 0 or 1.

The Diskin program examines the floppy disk in either drive A or B. Diskin then returns an errorlevel value from 0 through 2 based on the disk's condition:

Error Level	Meaning
0	The disk is formatted
1	The disk is unformatted
2	The disk is missing or the disk-drive door is open

To build DISKIN.COM, use your text editor to create the Debug script file shown in Figure 3-10. Carefully enter the instructions and save the file to disk as DISKIN.SCR. Be sure to double-check your work before saving.

```
n diskin.com
e100 A0 80 00 0A C0 74 09 A0
e108 82 00 24 5F 2C 41 EB 02
e110 B0 00 B9 01 00 BA 00 00
e118 BB 37 01 CD 25 73 12 80
e120 FC 1F 73 09 80 FC 08 74
e128 04 B0 01 EB 06 B0 02 EB
e130 02 B0 00 B4 4C CD 21
rcx
37
w
q
```

Figure 3-10. *The DISKIN.SCR Debug script.*

To create DISKIN.COM, enter the following at the MS-DOS prompt:

```
C>debug <diskin.scr
```

This builds the DISKIN.COM program, which you can then use to complete FORMAT.BAT.

To put FORMAT.BAT to work, place it in a directory in the path *before* the directory that contains the MS-DOS Format command. Then, when you enter *format* at the MS-DOS prompt, the smarter FORMAT.BAT file will be executed.

The first thing FORMAT.BAT does is use Diskin to test the disk in the drive. If the disk is already formatted, you'll be alerted with *That disk is formatted!*, and then you'll be asked if you want to continue. If you continue, the MS-DOS Format command formats the disk, and then control returns to FORMAT.BAT, which asks if you want to format another disk. FORMAT.BAT again checks to see if the disk is already formatted.

The idea here is to ensure that you don't accidentally format an already-formatted disk. Even given that MS-DOS 5 can revive such disks, precaution is best.

The FORMAT.BAT file isn't built to handle write-protected disks. If you try to format one, the Format command's error message is displayed, and FORMAT.BAT clears the screen (line 33) before you get a chance to read the error message.

You can modify FORMAT.BAT using the Getdrive command instead of the *if not %1!==!* test in line 2, with Getdrive asking for a drive to format. (Of course, any batch file can be modified to death; feel free to do so on your own.)

The following is the line-by-line description of the FORMAT.BAT file. You can skip to the section titled "Checking a Disk's Size Using the Disk-form Program" if you're not interested.

Line 1 turns the echo off.

Line 2 tests to see if FORMAT.BAT was followed by a drive letter. If not, the message *Specify a drive letter to format* is displayed in line 3, and the program quits by branching to the *END* label at line 42.

Line 7 calls the Diskin program, which examines the specified drive, %1. An errorlevel of 2 indicates that the disk is missing, which causes the program to branch to the *MISSING* label at line 22. An errorlevel of 1 indicates that the disk is present and unformatted, and execution branches to line 28. An errorlevel of 0 indicates a formatted disk, and execution branches to line 11.

Line 12 displays the message *That disk is formatted!* The Ask program in line 13 asks if you want to continue. If you press Y to continue, line 15 branches to the *FORMAT* label at line 30, where the disk is reformatted. If you press N to stop, the Ask command in line 16 asks if you want to format another disk. If you press N, execution branches to the *END* label at line 42. If you press Y, line 18 prompts you to insert a disk and the Pause command in line 19 waits for you to press a key. Line 20 branches back to the *START* label at line 6.

The program branches to line 22 when the Diskin program detects a missing disk or when the drive door is open. The Echo commands in lines 23 and 24 direct you to insert a disk in the drive; line 25 contains a Pause command that lets you press any key to continue. Line 26 then branches back to the *START* label at line 6, where the program re-examines the disk using the Diskin command.

The program branches to line 28 when it detects an unformatted disk. Line 29 displays the message *Unformatted disk detected.*

The program branches to line 30 when it detects a formatted disk and you signaled that it was okay to reformat the disk.

Line 31 displays the message *Formatting disk...*

Line 32 is the Format command, followed by any optional parameters (/S, /F, and so on). The /V parameter is specified here to give the disk the label "none." This circumvents the *Volume label* prompt Format would otherwise display. The ENTERN file supplies all the keystrokes the Format command requests: the Enter key for the initial *Press Enter when ready* message, and N for the *Format another?* prompt. Remember to specify the proper subdirectories for the MS-DOS Format command and the ENTERN file. If you have MS-DOS 3.3 or earlier, don't specify the */v:none* part of the Format command.

After formatting is complete, the batch file clears the screen in line 33. Line 35 asks if you want to format another disk. If you press N, line 36 branches execution to the *END* label at line 42. If you press Y, lines 37 and 38 display a message prompting you to switch disks. Line 39's Pause command waits for you to press any key. Finally, line 40 branches execution back to the *START* label at line 6.

Checking a Disk's Size Using the Diskform Program

The Diskin program shown in Figure 3-10 on page 51 reads information about a disk and returns the information to you in the form of errorlevel values. Diskin reports whether or not a disk is in the drive, and if so, whether or not the disk is formatted. Other information is also available, including information about the disk's formatted capacity and whether or not the disk contains files. Diskin skips over it, but the Diskform program shown in Figure 3-11 on the next page does not.

DISKFORM.SCR is a rather complex Debug script. It evaluates eight disk formats plus the presence or absence of files on each. Carefully type the commands shown in Figure 3-11 into a text file using a text editor. Double-check your work and save the file as DISKFORM.SCR. You create the Diskform program using the following MS-DOS command:

```
C>debug <diskform.scr
```

This command creates DISKFORM.COM, which you can then use to evaluate a floppy disk. Diskform returns 18 possible errorlevel values, as shown in Table 3-2 on the next page.

```
n diskform.com
e100 A0 80 00 0A C0 74 0D A0
e108 82 00 24 5F 2E A2 AB 01
e110 2C 41 EB 02 B0 00 B9 01
e118 00 BA 00 00 BB AF 01 CD
e120 25 73 04 B0 00 EB 7C 2E
e128 8A 26 C4 01 80 FC F9 75
e130 0E B0 0E 2E 80 3E C7 01
e138 09 75 45 B0 0F EB 41 80
e140 FC FC 75 04 B0 0B EB 38
e148 80 FC FD 75 04 B0 0D EB
e150 2F 80 FC FE 75 04 B0 0A
e158 EB 26 80 FC FF 75 04 B0
e160 0C EB 1D 80 FC F0 75 14
e168 B0 10 2E 80 3E C7 01 12
e170 74 0E B0 11 2E 80 3E C7
e178 01 24 74 04 B0 01 EB 23
e180 2E A2 A7 01 BA 80 00 B4
e188 1A CD 21 B4 4E BA A8 01
e190 B9 F7 FF CD 21 72 08 2E
e198 A0 A7 01 04 0A EB 04 2E
e1A0 A0 A7 01 B4 4C CD 21 00
e1A8 41 3A 5C 2A 2E 2A 00
rcx
af
w
q
```

Figure 3-11. *The DISKFORM.SCR Debug script.*

TABLE 3-2. DISKFORM'S ERRORLEVEL RETURN VALUES

Errorlevel	Meaning
0	Disk error
1	Unknown disk format
10	160-KB 5¼-inch disk, no files present
11	180-KB 5¼-inch disk, no files present
12	320-KB 5¼-inch disk, no files present
13	360-KB 5¼-inch disk, no files present
14	1.2-MB 5¼-inch disk, no files present
15	720-KB 3½-inch disk, no files present
16	1.4-MB 3½-inch disk, no files present
17	2.8-MB 3½-inch disk, no files present
20	160-KB 5¼-inch disk, files found
21	180-KB 5¼-inch disk, files found
22	320-KB 5¼-inch disk, files found
23	360-KB 5¼-inch disk, files found
24	1.2-MB 5¼-inch disk, files found
25	720-KB 3½-inch disk, files found
26	1.4-MB 3½-inch disk, files found
27	2.8-MB 3½-inch disk, files found

The Diskform program really does nothing by itself (although it does create a brief floppy-drive light show). To put it to work, you need a batch file. DISKCHK.BAT, shown in Figure 3-12, can be used to illustrate how well Diskform works. Create the batch file using a text editor or the MS-DOS Editor, and save the file as DISKCHK.BAT. (Use your text editor's Copy and Paste commands to make this process go faster.)

DISKCHK.BAT makes extensive use of errorlevel checking to test the value returned by Diskform (line 4). The *if errorlevel x if not errorlevel x+1* commands are used to narrow down the value returned by Diskform to the first number, *x*. DISKCHK.BAT displays a message telling you the disk's formatted capacity and whether or not it contains any files.

These programs are fairly heavy-duty, requiring more typing than most of the batch files or Debug scripts in this book. If you can work the results into other batch files (using the Call command), great! If not, evaluate the value of DISKCHK.BAT before you commit yourself to typing it.

You can add the Diskchk program to FORMAT.BAT to show the size of a formatted disk and whether or not it contains files. After line 12 in the FORMAT.BAT file, you could insert the following command:

```
call diskchk.bat %1
```

```
 1: @echo off
 2: if %1!==! goto ERROR
 3: echo Analyzing disk in drive %1
 4: diskform %1
 5: if errorlevel 27 echo A 2.8-MB, 3 1/2-inch disk containing files
 6: if errorlevel 26 if not errorlevel 27 echo A 1.4-MB disk containing files
 7: if errorlevel 25 if not errorlevel 26 echo A 720-KB disk containing files
 8: if errorlevel 24 if not errorlevel 25 echo A 1.2-MB disk containing files
 9: if errorlevel 23 if not errorlevel 24 echo A 360-KB disk containing files
10: if errorlevel 22 if not errorlevel 23 echo A 320-KB disk containing files
11: if errorlevel 21 if not errorlevel 22 echo A 180-KB disk containing files
12: if errorlevel 20 if not errorlevel 21 echo A 160-KB disk containing files
13: if errorlevel 17 if not errorlevel 18 echo A 2.8-MB disk without files
14: if errorlevel 16 if not errorlevel 17 echo A 1.4-MB disk without files
15: if errorlevel 15 if not errorlevel 16 echo A 720-KB disk without files
16: if errorlevel 14 if not errorlevel 15 echo A 1.2-MB disk without files
17: if errorlevel 13 if not errorlevel 14 echo A 360-KB disk without files
18: if errorlevel 12 if not errorlevel 13 echo A 320-KB disk without files
19: if errorlevel 11 if not errorlevel 12 echo A 180-KB disk without files
20: if errorlevel 10 if not errorlevel 11 echo A 160-KB disk without files
21: if errorlevel 1 if not errorlevel 2 echo Unknown disk format
22: if errorlevel 0 if not errorlevel 1 echo Disk error
23: goto END
24: :ERROR
25: echo Specify a drive letter with Diskform, either A or B
26: :END
```

Figure 3-12. *The DISKCHK.BAT batch file.*

The Call command executes one batch file from another—and returns to the first when the second is complete. The %1 variable is passed to DISKCHK.BAT as well. The end result is that the following messages are displayed when FORMAT.BAT tries to format an already-formatted disk:

```
C>format a:
That disk is formatted!
Analyzing disk in drive a:
A 1.2-MB disk containing files
Continue?
```

This makes the FORMAT.BAT program more informative, giving it a true professional edge.

Remember that MS-DOS versions 5 and later save special *unformat* information when a disk is reformatted; you'll usually be able to recover from accidentally formatting a disk. Fortunately, FORMAT.BAT and the other disk utilities in this chapter make the accidental formatting of a disk less likely to occur.

SUMMARY

By using simple MS-DOS tools such as batch files, plus the Debug utility, you can augment and extend the power of MS-DOS commands. You can also create improved versions of common MS-DOS commands such as Copy, Del, and Format, and create much-needed commands such as Move.

In addition, you can correct some problems with MS-DOS by patching. For example, it's easy to add or remove a beep from a program, as well as to create simulated MS-DOS commands using the Doskey keyboard enhancement tool. You can also patch COMMAND.COM itself, but this is only for the truly brave-hearted.

Finally, you've seen how working with floppy disks can be made easier using a few handy disk utilities and some powerful batch files. This gives MS-DOS more muscle than you ever knew was possible and makes working with floppy disks that much easier.

Chapter 4

Fine-Tuning
Your System

The world is full of modest solutions dedicated to helping you get the most from what you already have. Think of the schemes: real-estate investment opportunities that require "no money down"; health spas for improving your body; crystals, herbs, and moonbeams for your soul; and Geritol for your tired blood. People are always offering ways to make what you have work better. Computers are no exception, and—unlike the schemes above—these solutions won't cost you a dime.

This chapter shows you ways to improve your computer's performance. There's a practical limit here, though—no magic switch exists that shifts a PC into hyperdrive. (An old gag had PC wizards plugging their computers into 220-volt sockets to speed them up.) Instead, it's possible to improve your system's speed by removing some of the roadblocks and speed bumps that slow it down in the first place. The best part is that there's nothing to buy, no fancy hardware to invest in, no upgrades to install, and no speeches to sit through while you wait for a free toaster. You can take advantage of all the performance-boosting techniques in this chapter using only MS-DOS.

GETTING MORE SPEED
FROM YOUR HARDWARE

There are ways to improve the performance of certain parts of your PC, making those parts work faster (where the hardware allows) or using other techniques to shorten the time certain operations take. For example, you can adjust the speed of the microprocessor provided the hardware is designed to shift speeds. And you can use memory to boost disk-drive performance. The following sections detail these wonders and show how you can work them into your system.

Shifting into Turbo Mode

Some computers have a "turbo" switch, which you can use to toggle the computer's microprocessor between a slow, or "compatible," speed and its top speed. If your system has such a switch, it might be on the front panel, labeled *Turbo* or something similar. Some computers have a keyboard-activated turbo switch. Check your PC's manual to see if your PC has a turbo switch and to see how it's used on your system.

The turbo switch was introduced when "PC clones" began running faster than IBM-made originals. The slower speed allowed computers to run some programs (primarily games) that were far too fast at top speed. (For example, your little man would die because you didn't have enough time to kill the aliens.) Other programs, such as communications software, were timed to specific microprocessor speeds and were reliable only at those speeds.

Today, there isn't any reason to run a PC at the slow speed. Even games now adjust themselves to the speed of the computer, operating the same regardless of how fast your PC operates. So, if your computer has a turbo switch, *punch it up* and enjoy your system at its top speed all the time.

A Faster Disk Drive

Nothing beats buying a fast, large-capacity hard disk. If you don't want that expense, however, you can make your hard-disk drive work more efficiently by installing *disk caching* software. With MS-DOS, the caching software is provided by the SMARTDrive device driver. (I'll tell you more about this in the next section.)

A *cache* is a secret place for stashing things: nuts if you're a squirrel, jewels and booty if you're a pirate, guns and bombs if you're a terrorist, and sectors read from your hard disk if you're a computer user.

A disk cache retains a copy of data read from the hard disk, storing that information in memory. When MS-DOS or an application requests the same information from the hard disk again, the information is read from the cache's memory instead of from disk. Because the information is stored in memory, it's read much quicker than it would be from the hard disk.

Disk caches work because, typically, the same information is read from disk over and over. The cache keeps a copy of that information, so the more you access the hard disk, the more information is kept in the cache and the fewer times MS-DOS actually has to go out to the hard disk to get information. Disk performance increases the more you access the disk.

If you're familiar with the concept of a RAM drive, the disk cache may sound similar. However, a disk cache has several advantages over a RAM drive: There's no initial disk setup or copying involved; information from a number of drives can be cached using a single cache command; and because the cache keeps a copy only of data that is already on disk, no information is ever lost if the power goes out. Information written to disk still goes directly to the drive. Therefore, a disk cache is a risk-free method of improving disk performance.

Setting Up the Cache

MS-DOS provides disk-caching software, the SMARTDrive device driver (SMARTDRV.SYS). This is the same caching software that's available with Microsoft Windows 3.0. To use SMARTDrive, note that you need either extended or expanded memory.

To set up a cache with SMARTDrive, add a Device configuration command to CONFIG.SYS. Place that line after any other Device commands that deal with memory or setting up a hard drive. Here is the format:

   device=c:\ms-dos\smartdrv.sys *max min* /a

SMARTDRV.SYS is located in your MS-DOS directory. Be sure to specify a proper path to that location (C:\MS-DOS in this example).

The size of the cache is set by *max*, and it's measured in kilobytes. If *max* isn't specified, a 256-KB cache is created in extended memory. To place the cache in expanded memory, specify the /A switch. (For more information about extended and expanded memory, read the section titled "Working with Memory" at the end of this chapter.)

For example, to create a 512-KB cache in extended memory, you would use the following command in CONFIG.SYS:

```
device=c:\ms-dos\smartdrv.sys 512
```

You must specify the *min* value only if you're using Microsoft Windows version 3.0 or later and memory is tight. Windows has the ability to squeeze the size of SMARTDrive's cache memory down to *min* kilobytes, giving Windows programs more memory if necessary. Values for *min* range from 0, the default, to the value for *max*. If memory isn't a problem on your PC, and you want the cache always to remain the same size, specify the same value for *min* and *max*. For example:

```
device=c:\ms-dos\smartdrv.sys 128 128
```

In your CONFIG.SYS file, set a size for *max*, ensuring you have that much memory available. I suggest using 128 KB for starters, or 512 KB if you can spare that much memory. If necessary, set a size for *min*. Specify the /A switch if you want to put the cache in expanded memory, though I recommend keeping the cache in extended memory if at all possible.

Save your changes to the CONFIG.SYS file and then exit the editor. At the MS-DOS prompt, reset your computer.

When the system starts, you'll see the SMARTDrive startup message, telling you about the cache it installed. For example:

```
Microsoft SMARTDrive Disk Cache version 3.13
    Cache size: 512K in Extended Memory
    Room for 60 tracks of 17 sectors each
    Minimum cache size will be OK
```

To test the cache, perform a disk-intensive operation, such as the Chkdsk command. Enter the following at the prompt:

```
C>chkdsk *.*
```

Keep an eye on the hard-disk drive light to get a feel for how long the Chkdsk operation takes. (If you have a stopwatch handy, use it.) When Chkdsk is finished, enter the same command again (press F3 and Enter). You'll notice that the disk-drive light doesn't come on and the entire operation takes less time. That's the cache in action; the information Chkdsk needed was already in memory and read from the cache instead of from disk. You'll notice other speed improvements as you continue to use your PC.

Final Notes on Using a Cache

Your system needs only one disk cache. Unlike a RAM drive, which can be set up a multitude of times, you should have only one cache command in your system. If you need a larger cache, edit the command that sets up the cache to devote more memory to it.

When a cache is running on your system, reset the value of the Buffers configuration command to 20 (*buffers = 20*). Using any value higher than that wastes memory when SMARTDrive is running. If you're running Windows in conjunction with SMARTDrive, consider setting the Buffers command to 15.

If your system is set up with upper memory blocks (UMBs), you can load SMARTDrive high. Simply replace the Device configuration command with the Devicehigh command in CONFIG.SYS. However, doing this has been known to lock up certain types of hard drives. If you notice your system locking up suddenly, load SMARTDrive low instead. It takes up about 14 KB of memory, but remember that the cache memory is always located in extended or expanded memory.

You might also experience trouble with programs that do not cooperate with a cache. As more and more programs try to circumvent MS-DOS to get things done "more efficiently," problems arise with disk caches that expect MS-DOS's rules to be obeyed. The solution to this is simple: either disable the cache if you notice any problems, or find out which program is making waves and stop using it.

What About Fastopen?

The Fastopen command was introduced in MS-DOS version 3.3 as a type of cache. Fastopen remembers the last few filenames accessed, and it keeps a record of their locations on disk, making subsequent access to those files faster. It does not remember any information about the file's contents, nor does it read any sectors from disk.

If you're using SMARTDrive, you can dispense with Fastopen. If you have any extended or expanded memory in your system, I recommend that you use SMARTDrive instead of Fastopen. However, if you have only conventional memory, then consider using Fastopen. Here is the format for the Fastopen command:

    fastopen *drive*:=*n* ... /x

In this format, *drive*:=*n* is a disk-drive letter followed by an equal sign and a value ranging from 10 though 999; the default value for *n* is 48. Fastopen will keep track of *n* files on the specified drive. For example:

```
C>fastopen c:=100 d:=100
```

In this example, the Fastopen command remembers the last 100 files opened on drives C and D.

The /X switch puts Fastopen's data into expanded memory. Fastopen requires 48 bytes of storage for each file opened, so putting it in expanded memory can save on overhead.

You can put Fastopen in your AUTOEXEC.BAT file, or you can load it with CONFIG.SYS using the Install configuration command. For example:

```
install=c:\ms-dos\fastopen.exe c:=100 d:=100
```

I don't recommend using Fastopen. Use SMARTDrive instead. If you do use Fastopen, *do not* specify drives A and B—if you specify A or B, MS-DOS will refuse to let you swap disks in those drives, which can be annoying as all living hell.

Optimizing the Interleave

Another way you can improve the efficiency of a hard-disk drive is to optimize its *interleave factor*. That's a fancy term for the way sectors are arranged around a track. A proper interleave means the drive is working as fast as it can. If the interleave is wrong, it can take the hard-disk drive twice as long—or longer—to access information.

MS-DOS formats disks by laying down concentric rings, or *tracks*, of information. The tracks are further divided into 512-byte units called *sectors*, as shown in Figure 4-1. The typical hard disk has hundreds of tracks.

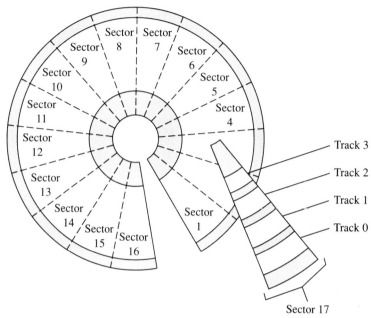

Figure 4-1. *Tracks and sectors on a hard disk.*

They're actually called *cylinders*, because tracks are located on both sides of a disk and a hard-disk drive can have more than one disk. Yet, no matter how many tracks or cylinders it may have, a typical hard disk has only 17 sectors on each track, with high-performance disks having 34 sectors per track.

These sectors are arranged around the track according to the interleave factor. For example, the interleave factor is 1:1 for a fast hard-disk drive. The sectors are then arranged sequentially, from 1 through 17, because the disk's controller can read them that fast. Figure 4-2 on the next page shows a 1:1 interleave factor.

Older hard-disk drives used a 3:1 interleave factor. In the time it took them to digest the sector just read, two other sectors rotated beneath the drive's read/write heads. To make disk reading efficient, the 3:1 interleave factor allows the next sequential sector to be positioned for reading—even though it may not be sitting next to the sector just read. (Figure 4-3 on the next page shows a 3:1 interleave factor.)

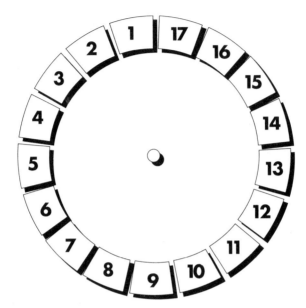

Figure 4-2. *A 1:1 interleave factor.*

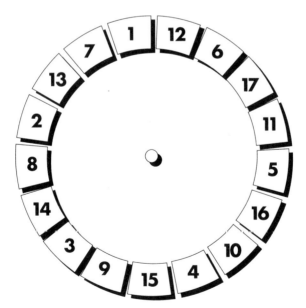

Figure 4-3. *A 3:1 interleave factor.*

Using a bad interleave factor, such as 1:1 for a disk that really requires 3:1, can dramatically slow a hard-disk drive. The drive has to wait for the proper sector to be in position before it can read the information. Granted, the wait is only a few microseconds. But it's wasted time; a better interleave factor can improve performance.

And now the bad news: MS-DOS can do nothing about the interleave factor. It's set when the hard disk is first formatted. The formatting program is a special low-level formatter—not the MS-DOS Format command. Using third-party utilities, you can check and reset the interleave factor, sometimes without reformatting the disk. This subject is addressed in Chapter 10.

DEALING WITH DISK FRAGMENTATION

MS-DOS tries to make the best use of disk storage. As new files are created, they're placed on the disk in sequential order, following files already on disk. Figure 4-4 on the next page shows how files are stored. You can assume that the files were added to the disk in this order: PROGRAM.COM, GO.BAT, BUDGET.BAK, BUDGET.XLS, and BIG.DOC.

MS-DOS keeps track of every file's location using the file allocation table (FAT), which is a map of the disk's storage space. A file's directory entry contains a cross reference to the FAT, which is how MS-DOS locates that file on disk. This system is efficient and works well for even enormous hard-disk drives. But it's not foolproof.

When you delete a file, it leaves a "hole." MS-DOS can use the space previously occupied by that file, filling in the hole with another file. This system works well for little files and for big files. When a little file is added, it can fit snugly into the hole left by another file. When you add a big file, however, it might need to be split to fit into one or more holes.

Figure 4-5 on the next page shows how one file, BUDGET.BAK, was deleted and replaced by a larger file, HUGE.DAT. The larger file is split in two pieces, or *fragmented*. Thanks to the FAT, MS-DOS can locate both pieces of the file; when you load such a file into memory, MS-DOS easily

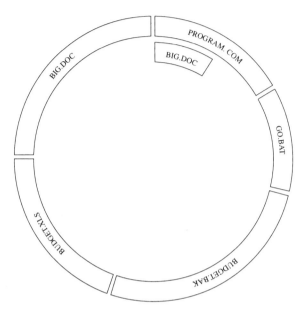

Figure 4-4. *Files are added one after the other to a disk.*

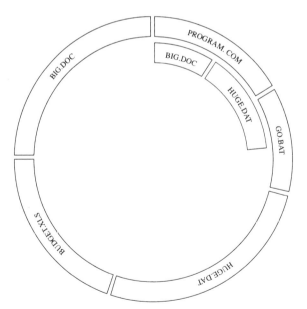

Figure 4-5. *The BUDGET.BAK file is deleted and replaced by HUGE.DAT.*

reassembles it. However, this takes extra time. The more fragmented files that you have on your hard disk, the slower the hard-disk drive's performance will be.

Checking Fragmentation

To check for fragmented files with MS-DOS, you can use the Chkdsk program. In addition to displaying disk information, Chkdsk can also tell you if any files are fragmented.

For example, to find out if you have any fragmented files in the root directory of drive C, enter the following command:

```
C>chkdsk c:\*.*
```

Chkdsk returns information in this format:

filename Contains *xxx* non-contiguous blocks

The *filename* is the name of the fragmented file, and *xxx* is the number of pieces. If you see the message *All specified file(s) are contiguous*, the directory has no fragmented files. (Pat yourself on the back.)

Checking for fragmentation with this approach has two flaws: The first flaw is that you must issue the Chkdsk command in each of your hard-disk drive's subdirectories to get a complete list of fragmented files. The second flaw is that, although Chkdsk reports fragmented files, there's nothing it can do about them.

A Fragmented File-Checking Batch File—with a Catch

You can get a list of fragmented files using Chkdsk and a special batch file. You could have the batch file change to each directory on your hard drive and issue the *chkdsk *.** command. However, it's easier if you have a file-sweeping utility, such as the Sweep program or the Global program. Then you can use that utility and the Find command to do most of the work. Figure 4-6 on the next page shows a program that locates fragmented files on a disk.

To use FRAG.BAT, you must have a utility like Sweep or Global. These utilities are available from local user-group libraries, bulletin boards,

```
1: @echo off
2: echo Checking disk...one moment please...
3: global chkdsk *.* >> \frags
4: cls
5: find /i "non-con" \frags | more
6: chkdsk | find "user"
7: echo Total fragmented files:
8: find /c "non-con" \frags
9: del \frags
```

Figure 4-6. *The FRAG.BAT program locates fragmented files on disk.*

national online services, or public-domain software warehouses. These
utilities repeat a specific MS-DOS command in each subdirectory on your
hard disk. In FRAG.BAT, Global is used in line 3 to repeat the Chkdsk
command across the hard disk. The results are then appended to the file
FRAGS in the root directory. This operation takes some time, and it usually produces a few *File not found* error messages.

Once the scan is complete, line 4 clears the screen. The Find command is
used in line 5 to sift through the FRAGS file for the text "non-con" (the
lines that list the files with noncontiguous blocks). The More filter is used
in line 5 in case the list of files is long and scrolls off the screen.

Line 6 displays the total number of files on the disk by finding the line
containing "user" in the Chkdsk command. That line usually reads something like this:

```
21906508 bytes in 736 user files
```

Line 7 then displays *Total fragmented files*, and the Find command is used
in line 8 to display the total number of fragmented files. The end result is
something like this:

```
----------- \FRAGS: 19
```

The Find command's /C switch displays a count of all lines containing
"non-con" in the FRAGS file. In conjunction with the number of total
"user files" on the disk, this should give you an idea of how fragmented
your hard disk is. The FRAGS file is then deleted in line 9.

Picking Up the Pieces

There's nothing wrong with fragmented files. MS-DOS keeps track of all
the pieces, so you'll never know if that document you just loaded is

fragmented on disk. (I would rather have a fragmented file on disk than have MS-DOS return a message such as *File too big*.) But too many fragmented files can make your hard disk seem like it's spinning in slow motion.

The only way to defragment files using MS-DOS is to completely back up your hard disk, reformat it (yes, *reformat* it), and then restore your files to the hard disk. This process lays down the files end-to-end, eliminating any fragmented pieces. Granted, this time-consuming task isn't something you'll want to do very often.

Third-party defragmentation utilities can pick up the pieces of fragmented files and make them contiguous. These utilities are covered in Chapter 10, and I highly recommend using one.

EXTRA CREDIT: REPARTITIONING A HARD DISK

One way to get more storage space on a hard disk is to repartition it. This isn't something I recommend for everyone. In fact, if your system was set up with MS-DOS 4 or later, you're probably using fairly large disk partitions already, so there's no need to repartition. If you've upgraded to MS-DOS 5 from an older version, however, you can benefit from repartitioning your hard disk—but only under certain circumstances.

For example, suppose you had a 90-MB hard disk divided into three logical drives, C, D, and E. Each drive stores 30 MB of information. Drive E is your Microsoft Windows drive and it's getting full. To recover some space, you could repartition your disk, taking a few megabytes away from drives C and D and giving them to drive E. Or you could make the whole disk one big 90-MB drive C and place your Windows files there.

Repartitioning to give your applications more hard-disk space is possible but not recommended. Unlike working with subdirectories, disk partitions are permanent, not to be messed with on a casual basis. You should consider repartitioning only if you truly need extra space.

Note: Before repartitioning your hard disk, it's a good idea to skip to Chapter 5 and create an Emergency Boot Disk.

If you decide to repartition a hard disk, here are the steps you take:

1. Back up all of your drives. Be sure you have your Emergency Boot Disk handy, along with a copy of your backup software. You'll need them to restore the hard disk.

2. Use the Fdisk program to delete all MS-DOS partitions on the hard disk. If you're connected to a network, log off before running Fdisk. Also, if you have more than one hard-disk drive, be sure you're working with the right one. If you do have multiple hard-disk drives, a fifth option for Fdisk appears, allowing you to switch drives. Figure 4-7 shows your choices.

   To delete a partition, select option 3, *Delete partition or Logical DOS Drive*. It may also read *Delete Logical DOS Drive(s) in the Extended DOS Partition* if you've changed to a second, nonbooting hard-disk drive. Press 3 and then press Enter.

   The next few screens will show you any logical drives in the partition. Type the letters for those drives you want to delete. You'll also need to enter the volume label and then press Y to verify. This effectively erases everything on all your logical MS-DOS drives.

   Press Esc a few times to return to Fdisk's main menu.

```
                        MS-DOS Version 5.00
                       Fixed Disk Setup Program
                   (C)Copyright Microsoft Corp. 1983 - 1991

                            FDISK Options

    Current fixed disk drive: 1

    Choose one of the following:

    1. Create DOS partition or Logical DOS Drive
    2. Set active partition
    3. Delete partition or Logical DOS Drive
    4. Display partition information
    5. Change current fixed disk drive


    Enter choice: [1]




    Press Esc to exit FDISK
```

Figure 4-7. *Fdisk's fifth option allows you to select another hard-disk drive in your system.*

3. Create the new partition(s). From the main menu, select option 1, *Create DOS partition or Logical DOS Drive.*

From the next menu, select either option 1 or 2: Option 1 creates a bootable MS-DOS disk, which should be the first partition on your first hard-disk drive. Option 2 creates an extended MS-DOS partition, such as you'd use on a second hard-disk drive (a data disk).

After creating the partition, or if it already exists, select Option 3 to create the logical drives in the partition.

Then comes the brainy part: You must divide the space on the hard disk into logical partitions, as shown in Figure 4-8. You can enter the size as a percentage of the total disk space, or you can enter the size in megabytes. If you use a percentage, follow the value with a percent sign (%).

If you want to use the whole disk as a logical drive C, D, E, or so on, enter *100%.* Otherwise, split up the disk using megabyte values or percentages. This will create logical drives on that partition.

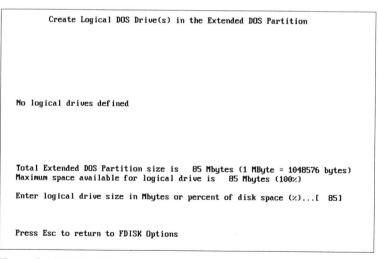

Figure 4-8. *Fdisk asks you to partition a hard disk by megabyte or percentage values.*

Note: If you don't know what value to use, simply press Enter. Fdisk is smart when it comes to partitioning a hard disk; the value it displays will probably work best for your system.

When you've finished, press Esc to return to the main menu. From there you can select Option 4 to review your partition information. Otherwise, press Esc to exit Fdisk. Your system will reset itself. (It needs to reset to load the new partition table into memory.)

If you've created a new primary MS-DOS partition, you must boot from an MS-DOS boot disk, such as the Emergency Boot Disk. Place the boot disk in drive A.

4. Format your new partitions using the Format command. For example, if you have repartitioned your second hard-disk drive and added a large disk D, enter the following:

```
C> format d:
```

You'll see the standard warning, alerting you that you're about to format a hard disk. Don't worry—nothing can be lost at this point. Press Y to format.

If you're formatting drive C all over, you might want to use the /S switch to reinstall MS-DOS and make disk C bootable:

```
C> format c: /s
```

Use the Format command on each of the other new hard-disk drives you created.

Note: If you get any weird error messages before formatting, such as Drive F: is write-protected, *rerun Fdisk. Use Option 4 to double-check your partition information. Then retry the formatting operation after quitting Fdisk.*

5. Finally, use Restore to restore the backed-up software and files to the hard-disk drive. This step is the most time-consuming part of repartitioning. You must restore each set of disks to the same drive, which might cause problems if subdirectories are similarly named.

Once everything is back safe and sound, re-run the *mirror /partn* command to update the PARTNSAV.FIL file on your Emergency Boot Disk.

Because you have repartitioned the disk, you must update PARTNSAV.FIL to help recover from any potential damage to your hard-disk drive's partition table.

WORKING WITH MEMORY

Working with memory is similar to incanting a spell. In many computer fantasy games you can unlock doors, move objects, and save yourself from certain peril, providing you know the right kind of mojo. Memory magic on a PC is similar, but you no longer need to be a computer wizard to put your memory to work.

Note: This book only touches upon the subject of memory management and putting memory to work. If you want an in-depth approach, see Microsoft Press' Managing Memory with DOS 5.

Memory in the PC

A PC can have four types of memory: conventional, upper, extended, and expanded. Each type of memory serves a different purpose and not every PC will have all four.

The most common and most important type of memory is *conventional* memory, the basic part of memory used by MS-DOS and your applications. It's limited to a maximum of 640 KB.

Above conventional memory, all PCs have *upper* memory. This starts at the 640-KB mark, right above conventional memory, and occupies 384 KB of space. That makes a total of 1,024 KB, or 1 MB, of memory in the basic PC configuration. Upper memory is used for various purposes: video memory, hard-disk controller, the PC's BIOS, and so on.

Any extra memory in a PC is either *extended* or *expanded* memory: Extended memory is memory beyond the 1-MB mark (above upper memory). This type of memory is only available in computers with 80286 or greater microprocessors. Expanded memory is any extra memory in a PC, but not memory above the 1-MB mark. Unlike extended memory, any MS-DOS computer can have expanded memory. Of the two types, expanded memory is more useful to MS-DOS applications, though Microsoft Windows gets more mileage from extended memory.

Managing Memory with MS-DOS 5

The goal of memory management under MS-DOS is to get as much conventional memory as possible. That can be done by using the special memory commands included with MS-DOS 5. The steps are:

- Controlling extended memory
- Loading MS-DOS high
- Creating upper memory blocks
- Loading high

This is complex stuff, but it's not difficult. The end result is more conventional memory available to your programs and to environments such as Microsoft Windows.

Controlling Extended Memory

You control extended memory on a PC using the MS-DOS HIMEM.SYS device driver. One command in CONFIG.SYS does the work:

```
device=c:\ms-dos\himem.sys
```

Once HIMEM.SYS is loaded, it controls extended memory by using the eXtended Memory Specification (XMS), and creates the High Memory Area (HMA), an extra 64-KB bank of memory that MS-DOS can use.

Note: HIMEM.SYS only works on 80286 or later PCs with at least 350 KB of extended memory.

Loading MS-DOS High

To load MS-DOS high, you use the Dos configuration command in your CONFIG.SYS file. For example:

```
dos=high
```

This command, in conjunction with the HIMEM.SYS device driver, loads MS-DOS into the HMA, freeing 50 KB of conventional memory.

Creating Upper Memory Blocks

The next step in MS-DOS memory management is moving device drivers and memory-resident programs out of conventional memory. You do this by creating *upper memory blocks,* or UMBs, and then using special commands to load device drivers and memory-resident programs into those special memory areas.

You create upper memory blocks by first adding the *umb* option to the Dos configuration command in your CONFIG.SYS file:

```
dos=high,umb
```

Next, load the EMM386.EXE device driver and specify either the *noems* or the *ram* switch; *noems* only creates UMBs, *ram* also creates expanded memory. If you need expanded memory, specify *ram,* as in:

```
device=c:\ms-dos\emm386.exe ram
```

If you don't need any expanded memory, such as when running Microsoft Windows, specify the *noems* switch:

```
device=c:\ms-dos\emm386.exe noems
```

Note: EMM386.EXE works only on 80386 and later PCs and only after HIMEM.SYS has been installed in the CONFIG.SYS file.

Loading High

After you create the upper memory blocks, you can transfer your device drivers and memory-resident programs into them. This is called "loading high," and you do it by using the Devicehigh command in CONFIG.SYS or the Loadhigh command in AUTOEXEC.BAT.

For example, the MOUSE.SYS device driver is loaded high using the *devicehigh* configuration command in your CONFIG.SYS file:

```
devicehigh=c:\mouse\mouse.sys
```

In your AUTOEXEC.BAT file, you load memory-resident programs high using Loadhigh. For example, the following loads Doskey high:

```
loadhigh c:\ms-dos\doskey /insert
```

You can also use Lh, the abbreviation for the Loadhigh command.

After you have made the changes to CONFIG.SYS and AUTOEXEC.BAT, you can use the Mem command to find out how much conventional memory is available. There will be plenty to run even the most demanding applications.

USING A RAM DRIVE

A RAM drive is a chunk of memory controlled by a special device driver. That device driver fools MS-DOS into thinking the memory is really a disk drive. MS-DOS assigns the "drive" a letter and lets you treat it like any other disk in your system: You can copy files to and from it, run programs and utilities on the RAM drive, put it on your network, and so on. But because the RAM drive is created in memory, it's much faster than any mechanical disk drive. By using the RAM drive, you can boost your system's performance, making some programs perform unconventionally fast.

MS-DOS comes with a RAM-drive device driver named RAMDrive. You install RAMDrive in CONFIG.SYS using the Device configuration command. The format is:

device=c:\ms-dos\ramdrive.sys *size sectors entries* [/e | /a]

Note: In some other versions of DOS, the RAM-drive software may be named VDISK.SYS.

The most important options for RAMDrive are the *size* option and the /E and /A switches. *size* sets the size of the RAM drive in kilobytes and ranges from 16 through 4,096, but it can be no greater than the memory in your system. If *size* isn't specified, a 64-KB RAM drive is created.

The /E and /A switches tell MS-DOS where to put the RAM drive. If you specify /E, the RAM drive will be created in extended memory; /A puts the RAM drive in expanded memory. Without the /E or /A switch, the RAM drive will be created in conventional memory, which is probably not what you want.

The following configuration command creates a 256-KB RAM drive in expanded memory:

```
device=c:\ms-dos\ramdrive.sys 256 /a
```

If you're using Windows or your system has only extended memory, use the following command instead:

```
device=c:\ms-dos\ramdrive.sys 256 /e
```

Putting the RAM Drive to Work

You can change to the RAM drive just as you would to any other drive on your system:

```
C>d:
```

All MS-DOS disk commands (except Format) work on the RAM drive, and you can use it as you would any regular drive.

The RAM drive is always given the next available drive letter in your system. So if you specify more than one *device=ramdrive.sys* command in CONFIG.SYS, you can create multiple RAM drives:

```
device=c:\ms-dos\ramdrive.sys 1024 /e
device=c:\ms-dos\ramdrive.sys 1024 /e
device=c:\ms-dos\ramdrive.sys 1024 /e
```

In this example, MS-DOS creates three RAM drives. Each is 1 MB (1,024 KB) in size and is created in extended memory. If your hard-disk drive is drive C, the RAM drives will be named D, E, and F. This lets you put a different type of program or set of data files in each RAM drive.

RAM Drive Techniques

The handiest purpose for a RAM drive is as a place for temporary files. To do this, set the MS-DOS Temp environment variable to the RAM drive in AUTOEXEC.BAT:

```
set temp=d:\
```

This technique works for Windows and for other programs that use the Temp variable.

If you download files, say from an online system or the office computer, you can copy them to the RAM drive to avoid any overhead caused by writing to a mechanical disk. Further, you can quickly uncompress compressed files on a RAM drive. But be sure to immediately copy anything worth keeping to a hard disk or floppy disk for permanent storage.

RAM drives are also excellent homes for demo programs (providing they aren't too big). Rather than waste space on a hard drive, if your RAM drive is big enough, install the demo there. The demo software will still work, and resetting will clear it away when you're done.

For optimization purposes, and to see a real increase in system speed, consider copying your batch-file directory to a RAM drive. MS-DOS accesses the disk twice for each line in the batch file. When the batch files are copied to a custom RAM drive, access time is drastically reduced.

As mentioned earlier, RAM drives are volatile. If you create any new files in a RAM drive or have files there that you want to keep, you must copy the files to a more permanent storage device before you reset or turn off your computer. Beyond that, RAM drives can be part of a winning solution to increase your PC's performance.

SUMMARY

There is no one switch to throw to put your system into top-flight mode. Instead, there are many little tricks you can do to enhance performance. These include adjusting your keyboard or display using the Mode command, setting up a disk cache or RAM disk, and dealing with file fragmentation. You can get more space on a hard disk by repartitioning it. This is an advanced technique, but it will give you more breathing room when space is tight.

Using the memory in your PC is another way to boost performance. Using MS-DOS 5, you can squeeze extra RAM from your system, as well as put extended and expanded memory to work.

Chapter 5

The Emergency Boot Disk

Running a computer isn't risky, at least not as risky as depicted in some popular science-fiction TV shows of the 1960s. When real-life computers die, they don't blow up, sparks don't shoot out, and robots don't walk out of your closet howling, "Crush! Kill! Destroy!" Still, the users on those TV shows were prepared for emergencies and, on the off chance that disaster strikes, you should be too.

This chapter begins a several-chapter discussion of safeguarding techniques. An interesting array of tools are available to assist with recovery from disaster (especially hard-disk recovery). But these tools won't do you any good sitting on a disabled hard disk. So a better plan—and one I highly recommend—is to create an Emergency Boot Disk. In fact, it's such a good idea that this entire chapter is devoted to getting yours started.

SETTING UP THE EMERGENCY BOOT DISK

An Emergency Boot Disk should contain important programs, tools for file recovery, and information files necessary for starting and rescuing a crashed computer. So that you can start the computer with the Emergency Boot Disk, it obviously needs to be a bootable disk.

Your Emergency Boot Disk should have the following items:

- A bootable copy of the operating system
- Custom CONFIG.SYS and AUTOEXEC.BAT files
- MS-DOS file-recovery and utility programs
- Third-party disaster-recovery and repair utilities
- Backup logs

Creating Your Emergency Boot Disk

To ensure that everything fits on your Emergency Boot Disk, obtain the maximum capacity disk for your A drive. (It must be for drive A, because that's the first drive the computer looks to when it starts.)

Follow these guidelines:

- If drive A is a low-capacity 5¼-inch drive, use a 360-KB disk.
- If drive A is a high-capacity 5¼-inch drive, use a 1.2-MB disk.
- If drive A is a low-capacity 3½-inch drive, use a 720-KB disk.
- If drive A is a high-capacity 3½-inch drive, use a 1.4-MB disk.
- If drive A is an extended-capacity 3½-inch drive, use a 2.8-MB disk.

The object is to use the largest capacity disk, one that will allow enough storage for all your recovery tools. If your drive A is a low-capacity 5¼-inch drive, you might need to create two Emergency Boot Disks, A and B.

Make a creative label for the Emergency Boot Disk—something along the lines of "Emergency Boot Disk" is okay, but you can use your imagination. The disk I use on my main computer has a classic Red Cross-like logo on the label.

Formatting the Emergency Boot Disk

After you've selected and labeled the disk, format it using this command:

```
C>format a: /s
```

Press Enter and follow the instructions on the screen.

When asked, give the disk the volume label *Useful*. There's no special reason for this, but when you use the *vol a:* command, you see:

```
Volume in drive A is USEFUL
```

Answer *N* when asked if you want to format another disk. (If you have only a low-capacity 5¼-inch drive, go ahead and format a second disk.)

If the disk shows any bad sectors, toss it out! Try again using another, maximum-capacity disk. You don't want to take any chances here.

Testing the Emergency Boot Disk

A lot of "getting MS-DOS right" involves testing things. There's no sense in being gung-ho about an Emergency Boot Disk if the word *Boot* is never put to the test.

With your freshly formatted Emergency Boot Disk in drive A, press the Reset button or press Ctrl+Alt+Del.

After a few spins of the second hand on your watch, your system should be up again—but booted from the floppy disk in drive A. (Booting this way takes longer because the floppy-disk drive is slower than your hard-disk drive.) You might see your system BIOS copyright message, plus a date prompt on your screen:

```
Current date is Tue 10-19-1993
Enter new date (mm-dd-yy):
```

If the date shown is correct, press Enter; otherwise, enter the current date. Do the same thing when the time prompt appears.

Eventually you'll see the MS-DOS copyright notice, and the A prompt will greet you:

```
Microsoft(R) MS-DOS(R) Version 5.00
          (C)Copyright Microsoft Corp 1981-1991.

A>
```

Ta-da! The Emergency Boot Disk works.

If none of this happens, or if you see a message such as *Bad or Missing Command Interpreter*, you probably have an older version of MS-DOS—one that doesn't copy the COMMAND.COM program to a boot disk when you use the *format a: /s* command. Remove the floppy disk from drive A and reset your computer again. When you see the C prompt, copy the COMMAND.COM file to the Emergency Boot Disk and test it again.

Moving On

All PCs can boot from drive A or from the hard-disk drive (C). Your system checks drive A first, primarily because all PCs are compatible with the original IBM model, which lacked a hard-disk drive. This compatibility has allowed us to do such things as create Emergency Boot Disks and have control over the computer when the hard-disk drive is out wandering in the garden.

Your computer is set up to run from the hard-disk drive. Two important files, CONFIG.SYS and AUTOEXEC.BAT, configure the system just the way you want it. Booting from drive A bypasses both of these files on the hard-disk drive, because MS-DOS checks for them on the boot disk in drive A instead. As a result (and because it's simply a good idea), you need to create custom CONFIG.SYS and AUTOEXEC.BAT files for the Emergency Boot Disk. Reset and, again, run your computer from the hard-disk drive by removing the Emergency Boot Disk from drive A and then pressing the Reset button or pressing Ctrl+Alt+Del.

Note: It's possible to go ahead and start your hard-disk drive from the A> prompt. Simply change to the hard-disk drive, like this:

```
A>c:
```

Then manually run AUTOEXEC.BAT, like this:

```
C>autoexec
```

You can't run the CONFIG.SYS file manually, which means that if the AUTOEXEC.BAT file assumes CONFIG.SYS has run (and set up memory, RAM drives, and so on), those programs probably won't work. That's why it's best to simply reset and restart your PC from drive C.

Creating Custom CONFIG.SYS and AUTOEXEC.BAT Files

The CONFIG.SYS and AUTOEXEC.BAT files you have in your computer probably took quite a while to perfect. They contain commands that customize the way your computer starts and runs, tailoring the computer's operation to the way you work.

You can copy your CONFIG.SYS and AUTOEXEC.BAT files directly to the Emergency Boot Disk, but you'll have to edit them to ensure that they reference programs, device drivers, and so on by a full pathname—including the drive letter (C:). But that's kind of pointless: If the hard drive is down, the commands won't work anyway.

Because the hard drive might be down, it's a good idea to copy all the programs, device drivers, and other utilities mentioned in CONFIG.SYS or AUTOEXEC.BAT to the Emergency Boot Disk along with CONFIG.SYS and AUTOEXEC.BAT. Then again, all those files are going to take up space that you might need for important recovery utilities. Will you really need ANSI.SYS, a mouse driver, RAM disks, or a pop-up appointment book when you're trying to revive a downed hard drive? Probably not.

Instead, do this: Copy your CONFIG.SYS and AUTOEXEC.BAT files to the Emergency Boot Disk, and then edit them aggressively. Remove the utilities you don't need; keep only the important files. You can really practice a little austerity here. These are the steps:

1. Put your Emergency Boot Disk into drive A.

2. Copy your CONFIG.SYS and AUTOEXEC.BAT files to that drive with these commands:

```
C> copy config.sys a:
        1 file(s) copied

C> copy autoexec.bat a:
        1 file(s) copied
```

3. Then edit the CONFIG.SYS file in drive A. Use your favorite text editor or the MS-DOS Editor, and be sure that you're editing the CONFIG.SYS file in drive A. For example, to use the MS-DOS Editor, enter the following:

```
C> edit a:\config.sys
```

(If you use a word-processing program, you must remember to save CONFIG.SYS as a text file when you finish.)

I'll leave most of the editing up to you. The primary goal is to cut out programs that aren't central to the recovery process. Here are some suggestions:

■ Delete any device drivers or programs loaded with the Device, Devicehigh, or Install configuration commands. Save programs that control, configure, or set up your hard disk—especially partition drivers, SCSI drivers, hard-card drivers, and other similar programs.

- Delete memory drivers. Keeping the HIMEM.SYS file is okay. Otherwise, retain memory drivers only if a recovery utility needs to access expanded memory.

- If you retain any device drivers or programs, edit their path-names, changing C: to A:.

- Remove the Shell configuration command; there's no sense in forcing MS-DOS to go on some wild goose chase for your COMMAND.COM file.

- Retain the Files, Buffers, and Stacks commands.

4. When you have finished editing the CONFIG.SYS file, edit the AUTOEXEC.BAT file on drive A. Use your favorite editor or the MS-DOS Editor. Here's the command for the MS-DOS Editor:

```
C> edit a:\autoexec.bat
```

As with CONFIG.SYS, keep only those programs that are central to the recovery process. Everything else can be deleted:

- Remove all memory-resident programs, except for those that con-figure your hard-disk drive. You can forgo mouse drivers, pop-up utilities, and other flash and dazzle.

- Remove recovery-preparation programs (such as Mirror), disk-optimization routines, and backup programs. Why? Because the hard-disk drive might be down or corrupted. At this stage, run-ning these programs can do more harm than good.

- Remove any commands that rely on RAM drives, and remove any elements that might no longer be set up in CONFIG.SYS. Don't bother using the Subst or Join command or any other command that affects the hard-disk drive.

- If you retain any programs or utilities, remember to adjust their pathnames to reflect their locations on drive A instead of on the hard-disk drive.

- Set the Path to only the root of drive A with this command:

  `path=a:\`

- You might want to change the prompt to the following:

  `prompt EBD$g`

  EBD stands for Emergency Boot Disk, and $g produces a greater-than sign (>).

- Don't worry about using the Set command to create other environment variables unless those variables pertain to recovery programs you put on the disk. However, the TEMP variable might be a good one to keep:

  `set temp=a:\`

- You can retain Doskey, though it will take up space on the disk (about 5 KB—not much).

- Cut out any shells or automatic startup programs at the end of AUTOEXEC.BAT.

Figure 5-1 below shows a sample CONFIG.SYS file before and after editing, and Figure 5-2 on the next page shows a sample AUTOEXEC.BAT file before and after editing. Although the edited versions of these figures are fairly safe bets for all PCs, remember that your changes should reflect your own system.

Before

```
REM MS-DOS 5 CONFIG.SYS file

dos=high,umb
device=c:\ms-dos\himem.sys
device=c:\ms-dos\emm386.exe noems

devicehigh=c:\system\mouse\mouse.sys /c1
devicehigh=c:\system\ms-dos\ansi.sys
devicehigh=c:\system\ms-dos\smartdrv.sys

files=32
buffers=32
stacks=0,0
```

After

```
REM Emergency Boot Disk

dos=high
device=a:\himem.sys

files=32
buffers=32
stacks=0,0
```

Figure 5-1. *CONFIG.SYS before and after editing on the Emergency Boot Disk.*

Before   After

```
@echo off                                       @echo off

REM set system variables...                     prompt EBD$g
prompt $p$g $a                                  path a:\
path c:\ms-dos;c:\win;c:\utility                set temp=a:\
set fastback=c:\fastback
set fbp_ems=500                                 doskey /insert
set temp=c:\temp

REM set your Doskey macros
lh doskey /insert

REM create f10 key for Doskey...
echo +[0;68;"doskey /macros";13p

win
```

Figure 5-2. *AUTOEXEC.BAT before and after editing on the Emergency Boot Disk.*

Copying Your Startup Programs

If you retain any programs in your Emergency Boot Disk's CONFIG.SYS or AUTOEXEC.BAT files, the next step is to copy them from your hard disk to the Emergency Boot Disk. For example, if you retained the HIMEM.SYS file, copy it from your MS-DOS subdirectory on drive C to the root directory on drive A:

```
C>copy \ms-dos\himem.sys a:\
        1 file(s) copied
```

If you retained Doskey, copy it as well:

```
C>copy \ms-dos\doskey.com a:\
        1 file(s) copied
```

In this example, the MS-DOS subdirectory is assumed; be sure to specify the correct subdirectory for your programs and commands when you copy them to drive A.

Copy any additional files as required. To verify that you have all the desired files, you might want to use the Type command on the CONFIG.SYS and AUTOEXEC.BAT files on drive A. Double-check that all files are loaded from drive A—not drive C.

When you're sure all the necessary files have been copied, test the Emergency Boot Disk again: with the disk in your A drive, reset your computer. The system should start right up. If you've changed your system prompt, as shown in Figure 5-2, you'll see something similar to the following:

```
EBD>
```

This is the Emergency Boot Disk's prompt, which lets you know that you've loaded the system from drive A.

If the test is successful, you can continue to create the Emergency Boot Disk. Remove the disk and reset your computer again to boot from the hard drive. (I promise, this is the last time you'll need to do this.) To continue creating the Emergency Boot Disk, skip to the section titled "Copying MS-DOS Programs and Utilities."

If any error messages appeared during this test, you should reexamine your CONFIG.SYS or AUTOEXEC.BAT files. Look for programs with inaccurate paths (all the files will be on drive A, so specify only A:\) and check for typos, or programs or files you've forgotten to copy to the Emergency Boot Disk.

You might want to print a copy of CONFIG.SYS or AUTOEXEC.BAT and make notes on the printout. To print either file, use one of the following commands:

```
EBD>copy config.sys prn
```

Or:

```
EBD>copy autoexec.bat prn
```

If you have a non-PostScript laser printer, enter this command to eject a page from the printer:

```
EBD>echo ^L > prn
```

Press Ctrl+L for the ^L character; don't type a caret (^) and an L.

After editing the file and fixing any errors, reset again to ensure the disk boots properly.

Copying MS-DOS Programs and Utilities

The next phase in creating the Emergency Boot Disk is copying important MS-DOS programs and utilities to it. I recommend those listed in Table 5-1 on the next page. Note that under versions of MS-DOS earlier than version 5, all of these files have a COM extension. Also note that Mirror, Undelete, and Unformat are available only with MS-DOS version 5 and later.

**TABLE 5-1. RECOMMENDED MS-DOS PROGRAMS AND UTILITIES FOR
YOUR EMERGENCY BOOT DISK**

Program	Filename	Function
Backup	BACKUP.EXE	Backs up files
Chkdsk	CHKDSK.EXE	Checks the disk and finds lost clusters
Debug	DEBUG.EXE	Debugging tool; helps initialize hard disks
Fdisk	FDISK.EXE	Partitions hard disks
Format	FORMAT.COM	Formats disks
Mirror	MIRROR.COM	Aids in recovering deleted files; backs up and restores partition table
Restore	RESTORE.EXE	Restores backed-up files
Sys	SYS.COM	Installs the system on a hard disk
Undelete	UNDELETE.EXE	Recovers deleted files
Unformat	UNFORMAT.COM	Recovers a formatted disk

If you have room for them, I also recommend that you copy Edlin (EDLIN.EXE) and the Mem program (MEM.EXE) to the Emergency Boot Disk. Edlin will come in handy as a text editor, should you need one; it takes up less room on disk than the MS-DOS Editor, which requires QBASIC.EXE (249 KB) to run. Mem is also an interesting tool, although it's not needed to recover a hard disk.

Copy each of the programs listed in Table 5-1 to your Emergency Boot Disk. Put them in the root directory of drive A; there's no sense in messing with subdirectories on a floppy disk.

After copying the files, there's no need to test the disk again—or from here on in. As long as it worked the last time you tested it, the disk is ready to be used in case of an emergency. Your only task is to complete the disk, which involves copying to it additional important programs and files as you read through this book.

Copying Third-Party Utilities

You should copy two other important utilities: your CMOS Setup program (if you have one) and any special hard-drive formatting or initialization programs.

The CMOS Setup program will access your system's battery–backed-up memory, allowing you to change or adjust it as necessary. (Some systems use a keyboard command to access a built-in Setup program.) If your system uses a Setup or similar program, be sure to copy that program to your Emergency Boot Disk.

If your system has a hard-drive initialization program, copy it to the Emergency Boot Disk as well. Hard-drive initialization programs could be named anything: HDINIT, HDSETUP, HSECT, WDFMT, and so on.

If you're using any third-party disaster-recovery programs or repair utilities, consider copying them, too. Chapter 10 lists some important third-party programs worth copying to your Emergency Boot Disk, including some gems from the Norton Utilities, PC Tools, the Mace Utilities, and other popular utility packages. Offhand, if you know of any must-have utilities, copy them now. But note that you don't need every program these utilities offer; copy only those programs central to the recovery process. Many third-party utilities include "bonus" programs that don't assist in disaster recovery.

This just about tops off what you can add to the disk; the MS-DOS utilities alone can take up 400 KB or more of disk space.

Creating a Special Disk for Third-Party Backup Programs

If you're not using the MS-DOS Backup program, there's no need to copy BACKUP.EXE or RESTORE.EXE to the Emergency Boot Disk. But you might want to copy to a separate disk any other backup programs you use. Consult your own backup program's manual to see which files are crucial to the recovery process. Then create a unique recovery disk for those files using the following Format command:

```
C>format a: /s
```

As you know, this command creates a bootable floppy disk. Be sure to use a large-capacity disk and label it your *Backup/Restore Disk.*

When formatting is complete, copy the backup program files necessary to restore the hard disk. (If the files won't all fit, consider removing some of the help files or any files not crucial to the restore part of the program.)

With the Backup/Restore Disk in drive A, reset your computer to be sure the disk works. If the disk doesn't boot, the COMMAND.COM file might be missing; reboot from your hard disk and copy COMMAND.COM to the Backup/Restore Disk.

If the Backup/Restore Disk works, reset your system again to boot from the hard disk.

Copying Backup Logs

Most third-party programs catalog their backup disk sets, noting which files are located on which disks. Cataloging aids the restore program in properly rebuilding the file structure on the hard disk, and in quickly re-storing single files or groups of unrelated files. If your hard disk crashes, restoration can only be done if you have a copy of the backup log on a floppy disk.

Note: The MS-DOS Backup program creates backup logs if you specify the /L switch. Most people don't bother with them. And besides, the backup logs aren't central to the recovery process as they are for some third-party recovery programs.

Copy backup logs for any third-party backup program to your Emergency Boot Disk. If you've created a unique Backup/Restore Disk, copy the backup logs there instead. Follow these guidelines:

■ For PC Tools's CP Backup, the log files have the extensions RPB or DIR. The names of the backup logs begin with the letter of the drive backed up and then have the date in a year-month-day format, fol-lowed by a letter of the alphabet. Generally, copying to the Emer-gency Boot Disk or Backup/Restore Disk all the DIR and RPB files that have the same filename will be enough.

- For FastBack, the catalog files have a filename that begins with the letter of the drive backed up and then have the year, month, and day, followed by a letter. Catalog files have the extensions VOL, FUL, INC, CPY, and DIF, though you probably need copies only of your FUL (full) backup logs.

- The Norton Backup uses catalog files with the extension CAT. Each backup set has a log filename that begins with two drive letters and then has the last digit of the year, the month, the day, and an alphabetic sequence letter. Backup sets have the extensions FUL, INC, DIF, and CPY.

Copying your backup catalog and log files is something you must do, especially after performing a full hard-disk backup. You should constantly update your Emergency Boot Disk or Backup/Restore Disk with the log files. Make it a part of your backup routine.

Is It Done Yet?

Nope. The Emergency Boot Disk is not complete yet. As you read through the following chapters, you'll be instructed to copy more programs and files to the Emergency Boot Disk. Appendix C summarizes my suggestions for which files to include on an Emergency Boot Disk. For now, you're off to a good start.

Keep the Emergency Boot Disk handy for additional fine-tuning and experimentation in upcoming chapters.

SUMMARY

You can use an Emergency Boot Disk to start your system in the event of a disaster. This disk provides a "clean" operating system plus a majority of the MS-DOS utilities that can aid in file or disk recovery. Keep this disk handy. And, to avoid the deterioration that comes with nonuse, copy the Emergency Boot Disk or Backup/Restore Disk to a fresh floppy disk at least once a year.

Chapter 6

Preventive Medicine

Most of the time we enjoy the luxury of stable, crash-free PCs. Crashes, bugs, and glitches seldom occur, so preparing for them is usually low on our priority lists. However, nothing beats the old adage, *An ounce of prevention is worth a pound of cure*. Being prepared is the hallmark of any experienced computer user.

This chapter introduces several important tricks you can perform *before* a crash—ways to prepare yourself and your computer in case the unthinkable happens. These tricks will help protect your data from being accidentally mutilated or erased and will assist in any recovery operations. Read these tips and follow the instructions carefully. That way, if a crash ever does darken your door, it's nice to know you've taken some extra steps to protect your data and your PC.

WHAT TO DO BEFORE A CRASH

Preparing for a computer crash is like preparing for an earthquake, volcano, tornado, or hurricane (depending on where you live): You have a first-aid kit handy, you've worked out emergency plans and maybe done a few drills, and you've made sure your house is firmly attached to solid ground. Then you wait and hope the disaster never comes. But if it does come, you're prepared.

Computer crashes can happen because of hardware failure. They might also be caused by strange doings on the power lines, errant mugs of coffee, misfortune, or carelessness. (For some reason, that commercial with the little kid feeding oatmeal into a VCR comes to mind....)

Just as you can prepare for a natural disaster, you can prepare for a computer crash or mishap. There are a number of things you can and should do. I have made a list of four basic preventive measures, all of which you can do using common, everyday tools you'll find lying around your computer:

■ Protect vital files

■ Preserve your hard disk with the Mirror utility

■ Back up your data

■ Care for your hardware

Each of these precautionary steps will keep your PC safe and aid in any recovery process. But like any preventive measure, never use them as an excuse to be negligent or careless. After all, no one sprays on shark repellant and then goes swimming with the chum.

Keep your Emergency Boot Disk, which you created in Chapter 5, handy for the exercises in this chapter. You'll need that disk for copying important system recovery files created by the Mirror utility.

Some of these protection tricks involve creating batch files. As I've said before, to be most effective, put all your batch files in a special batch-file subdirectory on your hard disk and place that directory in the path.

PROTECTING VITAL FILES

There are some files that you never want to mess with. For example, you don't want to rename, delete, or heckle COMMAND.COM, because without COMMAND.COM your system won't start.

In addition to COMMAND.COM, there might be other important system files, programs, or data files that you don't want to bother. For example, you might want to protect your AUTOEXEC.BAT and CONFIG.SYS files to prevent you from accidentally deleting them and prevent others—including certain installation programs—from altering their contents.

Files and Their Attributes

MS-DOS knows a file's name, its size, its date, and its secret location on disk. MS-DOS also keeps track of a file's *attributes*, which further describe the file. MS-DOS recognizes six attributes. One describes a disk's volume label and another identifies subdirectories. The other four pertain to ordinary files. These attributes are the following:

Code Letter	Attribute
R	Read-only
A	Archive (modified)
S	System
H	Hidden (invisible)

You can use the Attrib command to examine or alter any of the four attributes associated with a regular file.

When an attribute is turned on, or "set," that attribute has been applied to a file. For example, enter the following command at the MS-DOS prompt:

```
C>attrib c:\*.*
```

The Attrib command shows you a list of files in the root directory of drive C. At the left of each filename, code letters indicate which attributes are turned on for that file. For example, you might see something like this:

```
    SH        C:\IO.SYS
    SH        C:\MSDOS.SYS
A             C:\AUTOEXEC.BAT
              C:\COMMAND.COM
A             C:\CONFIG.SYS
         R    C:\WINA20.386
```

The *system* and *hidden* attributes are set for the two MS-DOS system files, IO.SYS and MSDOS.SYS. These attributes prevent the files from being displayed using the Dir command, as well as from being erased. The *archive* attribute next to a filename indicates that the file has been changed since the last backup was performed. No attribute next to a filename means that no attributes are set for that file.

In this example, the file WINA20.386 has its *read-only* attribute set, meaning that you cannot delete or modify that file. If you tried, you'd get an *Access denied* error message. Setting the read-only attribute for a file protects against carelessly deleting (or changing) the file. (You can copy a read-only file, but you can't delete it.) In effect, making a file read-only is like putting a padlock on it—a nice thing to have on an important file or program.

The LOCK.BAT File

You can slap read-only protection on any file, such as COMMAND.COM
or other important files you don't want messed with. You can protect files
with the Attrib command. Use this format:

   attrib +r *filename*

The +R after the Attrib command tells MS-DOS to turn on the read-only
attribute for the specified file or for a group of files if you use wildcards.

To quickly protect a file by setting its read-only attribute, you can create a
special batch file called LOCK.BAT. This batch file simply contains the
Attrib command shown above, but naming it LOCK gives it more stature,
makes it more memorable, and it gives you an opportunity to create a useful, system-enhancing batch file.

Create the following batch file using your favorite text editor or the COPY
CON command. Name the batch file LOCK.BAT and then place it in your
MS-DOS subdirectory or in a special batch-file directory in your path.

```
@echo off
attrib +r %1 %2
```

The first line turns echoing off. The second line uses the Attrib command
with the +R switch to turn on the read-only attribute of the specified file,
represented by the first variable, %1.

The second variable, %2, passes through the /S switch if you use it, which
makes the Attrib command turn on the read-only attribute of all matching
files in all subdirectories under the current directory. (The /S switch means
repeat this command for all subdirectories under the current directory. Its
meaning is fairly consistent for all MS-DOS commands.)

For example, to set read-only protection for COMMAND.COM, use the
following command:

```
C>lock \command.com
```

That's it. COMMAND.COM is now protected against being accidentally
deleted or altered. Go ahead: Try to delete it. You can't!

Do the same for other vital files on your system. For example, to lock all the COM files on your computer, use this command:

```
C>lock \*.COM /s
```

Starting with the root directory (\), Lock directs the Attrib command to lock all COM files (*.COM) in all subdirectories (/S) on the hard disk. You could do the same thing with all your EXE files, as well as with SYS files (device drivers):

```
C>lock \*.EXE /s

C>lock \*.SYS /s
```

Because you might need to remove the read-only protection at some point, here's the script for the UNLOCK.BAT batch file:

```
@echo off
attrib -r %1 %2
```

This is virtually the same batch file as LOCK.BAT, except for the -R after the Attrib command. As you'd suspect, -R turns off the read-only attribute for the file or group of files specified by the %1 variable.

Although locking files by setting their read-only attribute sounds like a smart thing to do, keep this in mind: A locked file has only a superficial form of protection. Some programs and disk utilities can still access the file, totally ignoring MS-DOS read-only security. And disk crashes can plow a hole right through a file easier than a hot knife cuts through butter. However, to protect against carelessness, bugs, and minor program burps, setting read-only protection with the LOCK.BAT program is wonderful.

Note: You might notice that LOCK.BAT and UNLOCK.BAT contain no error checking. That's okay: Any error messages produced by a nonexistent or bad filename will be generated by the Attrib command itself; the batch file doesn't need to check for errors.

Hiding Files

You can also use the Attrib command to hide files, although this is more of a form of file security—keeping sensitive files out of sight—than it is a file-protection technique. Locking your files with read-only protection is enough to prevent them from being accidentally modified or deleted.

However, if you do want to go around hiding files, here's a script for the HIDE.BAT file:

```
@echo off
attrib +h %1 %2
```

The +H switch hides the file. There's no fanfare involved; the file simply will be invisible to the standard Dir command and ignored by all MS-DOS commands that use *.* or any matching wildcards.

Note that hidden files are easily found under two circumstances. First, you can use the /A switch with the Dir command to list all files, even the invisible ones. (Or you can use the /A:H switch to list only invisible files.) And second, if you know the exact name of an invisible file, you can use it with any MS-DOS command or access it from within any program. Hiding files is another form of casual—but not foolproof—protection.

Here is the UNHIDE.BAT file, used to make a hidden file visible:

```
@echo off
attrib -h %1 %2
```

A Handy Trick for Saving CONFIG.SYS and AUTOEXEC.BAT

Sometimes, locking CONFIG.SYS or AUTOEXEC.BAT can be a pain. If you're like me, you modify these files about once a month, constantly tuning and tweaking them. There's nothing wrong with that, but locking and unlocking files is time consuming when you modify them frequently.

A better solution is to create backup CONFIG.SYS and AUTOEXEC.BAT files. You can do this using the following two Copy commands in the last part of your AUTOEXEC.BAT file:

```
copy \config.sys \temp > nul
copy \autoexec.bat \temp > nul
```

These two Copy commands create duplicates of the CONFIG.SYS and AUTOEXEC.BAT files, putting them in a TEMP subdirectory on disk. If TEMP doesn't exist, you must create it. Otherwise, specify a temporary subdirectory or use your MS-DOS directory. Or better still, use the TEMP environment variable if you've defined one:

```
copy \config.sys %temp% > nul
copy \autoexec.bat %temp% > nul
```

The > *nul* part of the command redirects the message *1 file(s) copied* to the NUL device, which makes the batch file run with a clean display.

Beyond File Security: Using Password Protection

A really nifty way to protect files, or your hard disk in general, is to apply a password. Only people who know the password can access the file or your hard-disk drive. Quite a few third-party utilities exist that set passwords, and some applications will let you password-protect (or encrypt) their data files for security. But MS-DOS doesn't provide this type of effective security.

MS-DOS does have convoluted ways that you can use to create menu systems and apply passwords using batch files. Most of these methods are easily defeated, however, because anyone who can use the Type command can see the contents of a batch file. Even the MS-DOS Shell, which offers some password protection, can be circumvented by a knowledgeable user. (And the MS-DOS Shell passwords are openly visible in the DOSSHELL.INI file.)

Someday MS-DOS might offer password protection as a way to secure files and prevent them from being accidentally changed or deleted. Until then, look into third-party file security routines, password schemes in both hardware and software, and data encryption for your security needs.

PRESERVING YOUR HARD DISK WITH MIRROR

Beginning with version 5, MS-DOS comes with a handy disaster prevention and recovery utility, Mirror. Two of the Mirror's preventive features, the partition saver and disk system-area saver, will help you recover from major disk catastrophes. A third preventive feature, deletion tracking, helps you recover accidentally deleted files.

Using Fdisk to Examine Your Hard Disk's Partition Information

When your PC starts, it actually boots your hard disk twice. The first time, it loads the disk's true boot sector, which contains a *partition table*. This table describes how the disk is divided up or *partitioned*. Loading it is central to getting your hard disk running.

For example, your 100-MB hard disk might be 100 percent dedicated to MS-DOS and partitioned as a full 100-MB drive C. Or 10 percent could be devoted to another operating system (say, XENIX) and the rest split three ways to MS-DOS: first as a 30-MB bootable drive C, then as two 30-MB "logical" drives, D and E. All this information is kept in the partition table, which is the first physical sector on the hard disk. The PC loads this information when it starts and then continues loading information based on which partition is flagged as the boot partition (MS-DOS in this case).

How you divide your hard disk is up to you. Ordinarily, you'll simply dedicate the whole disk to MS-DOS and then divide it (or not divide it) as you see fit. You can review how your own disk is partitioned by using the Fdisk command. At the MS-DOS prompt, type *fdisk* and press Enter.

```
C>fdisk
```

You'll see something similar to Figure 6-1.

Note: You cannot run Fdisk while your system is connected to a network. If you see an error message to that effect, log off from your network and run Fdisk again.

To see a summary of your disk's partition information (essentially a description of the boot sector), select item 4 by pressing 4 and then Enter. You'll see information similar to Figure 6-2.

If you have more than one partition, all of them will be listed. In Figure 6-2, the entire 40-MB disk is a single partition, drive C. It's the primary MS-DOS partition (PRI DOS), the boot disk. Extended or non-booting MS-DOS partitions are labeled "EXT DOS."

To exit Fdisk and return to the MS-DOS prompt, press Esc twice.

```
                         MS-DOS Version 5.00
                       Fixed Disk Setup Program
                  (C)Copyright Microsoft Corp. 1983 - 1991

                           FDISK Options

Current fixed disk drive: 1

Choose one of the following:

1. Create DOS partition or Logical DOS Drive
2. Set active partition
3. Delete partition or Logical DOS Drive
4. Display partition information


Enter choice: [1]




Press Esc to exit FDISK
```

Figure 6-1. *Fdisk's main menu.*

```
                    Display Partition Information

Current fixed disk drive: 1

Partition  Status    Type    Volume Label  Mbytes   System   Usage
  C: 1        A     PRI DOS    MS-DOS 5       40     FAT16     98%


Total disk space is    41 Mbytes (1 Mbyte = 1048576 bytes)




Press Esc to continue
```

Figure 6-2. *Fdisk's partition information.*

Warning: *Be careful with Fdisk! It creates as well as destroys partitions on the hard disk. Damage done here can be irreparable, so this is not the time to experiment.*

Saving the Hard Disk's Partition Information

Obviously, the partition information is a crucial part of the disk. Even on the largest hard disk, if that 512-byte-long sector is damaged, the rest of the disk is useless. A cornerstone of the Mirror utility is that it can take that important information stored in the partition table and store it in a file on a floppy disk. That way, if anything ever happens to those significant 512 bytes, you can restore your partition table and your hard disk with one simple command.

To save your hard disk's boot sector, use the Mirror command with its /*partn* (for partition) switch. Type the following at the MS-DOS prompt:

```
C>mirror /partn
```

You'll see the following message:

```
Disk Partition Table saver.

The partition information from your hard drive(s) has been
read.

Next, the file PARTNSAV.FIL will be written to a floppy
disk.  Please insert a formatted diskette and type the name
of the diskette drive.
What drive? A
```

Insert your Emergency Boot Disk in drive A. Press Enter. When the operation is complete, the word *Successful* appears on the screen.

The Mirror utility reads all the partition-table information from the boot sectors of every hard drive in your system and writes that information to a file named PARTNSAV.FIL, which is now on your Emergency Boot Disk. Should anything ever happen to your hard disk's boot sector, you can use the Mirror command to repair it. (Hard-disk problems are covered later, in Chapter 8.)

This procedure needs to be done only once—and you've just done it. Only if you add a new hard-disk drive to your system, or if you change your partition information using Fdisk, will you need to use *mirror /partn* again.

You can put your Emergency Boot Disk back in a safe place for now. But keep it handy; you'll use it again soon.

Saving the System Area

Aside from a hard disk's partition table, the most important items on any disk are the boot sector, the file allocation tables (FATs) and the root directory. The boot sector is responsible for loading MS-DOS (on a boot disk); the FAT is a map telling MS-DOS where all your files are located; and the root directory is the main directory on the disk. If any one of those three items is missing or damaged, the rest of the information on the disk will be next to useless. But, never fear—Mirror comes to the rescue.

As its name suggests, Mirror can create a mirror image of the boot sector, FAT, and root directory on any disk. That image—the system area—is then kept in a file named MIRROR.FIL in the root directory.

This is the Mirror command format that saves the system-area image:

mirror *drive* [/1]

In this command, *drive* is a disk-drive letter, followed by a colon. Mirror creates a MIRROR.FIL file for the system area on that drive. For example:

```
mirror c:
```

This command causes Mirror to create a MIRROR.FIL file for the boot sector, FAT, and root directory of drive C. You'll see the following information displayed:

```
Creates an image of the system area.
Drive C being processed.

The MIRROR process was successful.
```

To protect more than one drive, specify each of their names after the Mirror command:

```
mirror c: d: e:
```

In this example, drives C, D, and E are all protected by Mirror.

The /1 (one, not a lowercase L) switch prevents Mirror from making a backup of any older MIRROR.FIL files. If you don't specify this switch, any existing MIRROR.FIL file is renamed MIRROR.BAK when you run Mirror. The new information is then saved in the new MIRROR.FIL file.

To make the most effective use of the MIRROR.FIL file, it should be updated often to reflect changes on your disk—especially stuff that would show up in the FAT or root directory (which is just about everything).

The best way is to put the Mirror command for your system into your AUTOEXEC.BAT file.

Using your text editor or the MS-DOS Editor, edit AUTOEXEC.BAT; add the proper Mirror command for your PC. For example, my laptop has a single hard-disk drive, so I'll add this command:

```
mirror c: /1
```

My desktop PC has six hard-disk drives, C through H. Here's that system's Mirror command in AUTOEXEC.BAT:

```
mirror c: d: e: f: g: h: /1
```

In both examples, the /1 switch keeps only one copy of MIRROR.FIL on the disk and saves about 50 KB of disk space. I recommend using it.

Customize the Mirror command in your PC's AUTOEXEC.BAT accordingly. Specify all your hard-disk drive letters. Save your AUTOEXEC.BAT file back to disk. (You might need to unlock it first, if you locked it earlier in this chapter.)

To keep the MIRROR.FIL file up to date, you should reset your system at least once a week, if not more often. (You don't have to reset; simply turning your system on in the morning will do the job.) If your PC can't be reset, simply run the proper Mirror command at the MS-DOS prompt once a week. Or, better still, create a custom Mirror batch file. I call mine IMAGE.BAT:

```
@echo off
rem program to run Mirror once a day (because I don't reset)
mirror c: d: e: f: g: h: /1
```

If you use Mirror often, and if anything ever happens to the boot sector, FAT, or root directory, or if the entire disk is accidentally formatted, you can use the MS-DOS Unformat command to fully recover your disk. Thanks to MIRROR.FIL, the recovery process is smooth and quick.

Note: Perhaps you've noted a bit of irony—if the root directory is damaged, how can you recover the disk when the MIRROR.FIL file is in the root directory? The secret is that the file itself is stored at the end of a disk. If you need to recover the disk, the Unformat command knows where to look for MIRROR.FIL and can recover everything else from there.

Protecting Files with Mirror's Deletion Tracking

Mirror's third safeguard comes in the form of deletion tracking—keeping track of deleted files to help you recover them.

The Mirror utility becomes memory resident when you turn on deletion tracking. Mirror sits high in RAM and watches for the nasty Del or Erase commands. When you use one of these commands to delete a file, Mirror makes copious notes about the file's name, its location, and so on, and keeps this information in a special hidden file, PCTRACKR.DEL, in the root directory of the disk. If you need to restore a recently deceased file, the Undelete command will scan PCTRACKR.DEL, which makes file recovery a cinch.

You can turn on deletion tracking at the same time you're using Mirror to save a drive's system image. Here's the format:

mirror /t*drive*[*-files*]

Mirror activates deletion tracking for all files on the disk represented by *drive*—which should *not* be followed by a colon. For example:

```
mirror c: /tc
```

The Mirror command shown above might find a place for itself in your AUTOEXEC.BAT file. Mirror initially makes a system-area image for drive C; it then activates deletion tracking for that same drive.

If you want Mirror to activate deletion tracking for more than one drive, you must specify a /T switch for each drive. Here's an example of a command you could use in AUTOEXEC.BAT to protect multiple drives:

```
mirror c: d: /tc /td
```

A system-area image is made of both drives C and D, and deletion tracking is activated for both drives via two /T switches.

The optional *-files* value determines the number of files that deletion tracking will monitor. If you don't specify a value, Mirror creates a PCTRACKR.DEL file based on the size of the drive—for a 32-MB drive, Mirror would create a 36-KB file capable of storing information on up to

202 deleted files. The size is always keyed to the size of the disk drive, as shown in Table 6-1.

TABLE 6-1. MIRROR'S PCTRACKR.DEL FILE SIZE BASED ON DISK CAPACITY AND -*FILES* VALUE

Disk Capacity	-*files* (Default)	PCTRACKR.DEL Size
360 KB	25	5 KB
720 KB	50	9 KB
1.2 MB	75	14 KB
1.4 MB	75	14 KB
32 MB	202	36 KB
32 MB	303	55 KB

I recommend always setting the -*files* value to 100. This keeps the size of the PCTRACKR.DEL file down to about 18 KB max. Only if you think you might disastrously delete more than 100 files in one fell swoop—and want them all back—should you specify a higher value (see Table 6-1) or no value.

Here is the final Mirror command you might want to add or edit in your AUTOEXEC.BAT file:

```
mirror c: /tc-100 /1
```

With deletion tracking turned on, undeleting files is easier. (You can still undelete files without it, but it's awkward.) When you reset or turn the system on, you'll see a message similar to the following displayed:

```
Creates an image of the system area.

Drive C being processed.

The MIRROR process was successful.

Deletion-tracking software being installed.

The following drives are supported:
Drive C - 100 files saved.
Installation complete.
```

In its deletion tracking mode, Mirror is memory resident—and smart. If you've created upper memory blocks, Mirror will automatically load itself there; you don't need to use the Loadhigh command. (For more information on upper memory blocks and the Loadhigh command, read Microsoft Press's *Managing Memory with DOS 5*.)

To remove Mirror from memory and turn off deletion tracking, use Mirror with the /U switch. This frees up the 6.4 KB of memory Mirror uses. But be careful: Remove Mirror only if there are no memory-resident programs loaded after it.

BACKING UP YOUR DATA

It goes without saying that backing up your hard disk is a major bother. I'll be brief, but I have to say it anyway: You should have, as part of your regular computer regimen, some type of backup schedule. Design one and stick to it. The reason is simple: Nothing provides better damage control than having a duplicate copy of all your programs and files—your entire hard disk—sitting on one or two sets of backup disks.

You can use the MS-DOS Backup command or some third-party program to back up your hard disk. You can use floppy disks or a tape drive (if you have one). Just back up your disk and stick to your schedule. (Sometimes it takes a major disk crash to make you appreciate backing up. It did me. I lost three months' worth of work. I hope it never happens to you.)

Making Regularly Scheduled Backups

Part of the mental stigma of backing up is that it takes time. True, it does. It also takes time to strap fidgeting Junior into his car seat, but you do it anyway. The secret to both is having a plan of attack.

Daily

I recommend doing one of two types of backup every day: a work backup, which could simply mean copying your current working directory on a floppy disk, or an incremental backup, backing up all the files you created or modified during the day.

My daily backup is a work backup—a backup of the subdirectory that contains all the files for whatever project I'm working on. BACK.BAT, the batch file shown on the next page, does the job.

```
@echo off
backup d:\books\hotline a: /s
```

BACK.BAT backs up all the files from the BOOKS\HOTLINE directory—
and all its subdirectories, as indicated by the /S switch—to the disk in
drive A. This program takes maybe 20 seconds to run at the end of the day.

A daily incremental backup would copy all the files you've changed or
modified to a floppy disk. For example, if today is Wednesday, find your
daily-backup disk labeled "Wednesday," put it in the drive, and then use
the following Backup command:

```
C>backup c:\ a: /s /m
```

This Backup command backs up all the files in drive C in all subdirectories. The /M switch, however, directs Backup to copy only those files that
have their archive' attributes set. Depending on how much work you do,
this could take maybe two minutes of your time.

*Note: If you have more than one hard-disk drive, you should use the
Backup command on each of them; in the example here, replace* C: *with
the proper drive letter and colon.*

Weekly

You should do one of two types of backup every week: either a full hard-
disk backup or a full incremental backup. Choosing one depends on how
you do your daily backups.

If you do daily backups of only your work files, do a weekly incremental
backup. This will catch all those files you've worked on, changed, or
modified outside of your work subdirectory.

Obtain a disk for a certain week in the month. For example, this is the 15th
of the month and it's the third week of the month. Grab your third week's
backup disk set and enter the following command:

```
C>backup c:\ a: /s /m
```

This Backup command archives all modified files on drive C to a floppy
disk in drive A (or to more than one disk if there are many files). Remember to back up hard-disk drives other than C: if necessary.

If you do a daily incremental backup, then do a full hard-disk backup at the end of each week. Here is the Backup command to use:

```
C>backup c:\ a: /s
```

Without the /M switch, Backup creates an archive of all files on the specified hard-disk drive. Remember to back up all the other hard-disk drives in your system as well.

Monthly

If you're not doing a weekly full backup, take the time to back up your entire hard disk once a month. Use the same Backup command as for a weekly full backup.

If you follow a schedule similar to the one described here, backing up will take a minimum of time and you'll always be certain to have a safety copy of your data. Not even the smartest hard-disk recovery tool is a substitute for a backup copy of your files.

Checking Before an Incremental Backup

What makes an incremental backup work is the archive attribute MS-DOS puts on those files that have been changed since the last backup. The Backup program switches off the archive attribute for each file it backs up. If MS-DOS creates a new file or modifies an existing one, that file's archive attribute is switched on when you save the file. This is how the Backup command with the /M switch (and third-party backup programs) can identify un-backed-up files.

You can also use the Attrib command to locate files that have their archive attributes set. But rather than wade through that muddle, consider using the ARCHIVE.BAT batch file shown in Figure 6-3.

```
1: @echo off
2: rem located and tally files to be backed up
3: echo Scanning files to back up...
4: %1
5: cd \
6: attrib *.* /s > tally
7: echo You need to back up this many files:
8: find /c "A " tally
9: del tally
```

Figure 6-3. *The ARCHIVE.BAT program.*

Create this batch file program using your text editor or the MS-DOS Editor. Be sure to type a capital *A* followed by a space enclosed in quotation marks for the Find command. Save the file as ARCHIVE.BAT.

When you run the ARCHIVE.BAT file, it scans the files on the current hard-disk drive and gives you a total count of the files modified since the last backup. This, in turn, gives you an idea of how necessary an incremental—or full—backup is. For example:

```
C>archive
Scanning files to back up...
You need to backup this many files:

---------- tally: 35
```

As you can see, a total of 35 files have been modified since the last backup. You can also follow the Archive command with a drive letter to check files on a specific drive:

```
C>archive d:
Scanning files to back up...
You need to backup this many files:

---------- tally: 342
```

Whoa! Time to back up.

Here is a description of how ARCHIVE.BAT works:

Line 1 contains the initial Echo off command. Line 2 is a Rem command, describing what the batch file does. Line 3 echoes the message *Scanning files to back up...*

Line 4 contains the command-line variable %1. This changes to any drive letter, C:, D:, or whatever follows *archive* at the MS-DOS prompt. Line 5, Cd \, changes to the root directory of the drive specified in line 4.

Line 6 runs the Attrib command, scanning all files on the hard-disk drive. The output is redirected to a file named TALLY. In line 7, the message *You need to backup this many files* is echoed to the display.

Line 8 uses the Find command with the /C, or *count*, switch. This displays a count of all the lines that contain a capital *A* followed by a space in the output of the Attrib command, effectively counting only those files with their A, or archive, attribute set.

Finally, line 9 deletes the TALLY file.

Using Backup Disk Sets

When you back up your system, it helps to have enough disks handy. To make the best use of your hardware, use the highest-capacity disks allowed for your drives. Also use high-quality disks; you definitely don't want to skimp on something as important as a backup.

To figure out how many disks you'll need, you can use the Chkdsk command. Chkdsk reports the amount of disk space used by all files on your system. Divide that amount by the size of a single backup disk and you'll know how many disks you'll need. For example:

```
C>chkdsk
Volume MS-DOS 5     created 09-21-1992 1:26p
Volume Serial Number is 16CE-9B67

  42366976 bytes total disk space
     77824 bytes in 4 hidden files
    100352 bytes in 47 directories
  25159680 bytes in 841 user files
  17029120 bytes available on disk

      2048 bytes in each allocation unit
     20687 total allocation units on disk
      8315 available allocation units on disk

    655360 total bytes memory
    637616 bytes free
```

Look for the value *bytes in xxx user files* (in this example, 25,159,680). Divide the *bytes in xxx user files* value by 1,024—the number of bytes in one kilobyte (in this example, 25,159,680/1,024 = 24,570). Then to figure out how many backup disks you'll need, divide that value by the appropriate value from Table 6-2 on the next page.

For example, if you're backing up to 1.2-MB floppies, you will need 21 disks (24,570/1200 = 20.475). If you have 2.8-MB disks, you will need only 9 disks (24,570/2,800 = 8.775).

**TABLE 6-2. VALUES YOU CAN USE TO DETERMINE
THE SIZE OF BACKUP DISK NEEDED**

For This Size Disk	Use This Value	For This Size Disk	Use This Value
360 KB	360	1.4 MB	1400
720 KB	720	2.8 MB	2800
1.2 MB	1200		

Before you begin a backup procedure, number the disks. You don't need to format the disks, but numbering them (from 1 through x) will help you keep them in order for any eventual restore operation (see Chapter 8).

Label the first disk in the set to describe what type of backup it contains: daily, monthly, full, incremental, work, Monday, Tuesday, and so on. Also, if you're backing up to more than one disk set, label the sets accordingly. For example, if you have two sets of disks for full disk backups, label them A and B, Odd and Even, Yin and Yang, and so on.

Keep your disk sets in a safe place when you're not using them. You don't want someone to assume they're freebie disks that can be used for just anything.

Backing Up to a Tape Drive

If you're lucky enough to have a tape drive in your system, backing up is a snap. Usually, the tape drive will come with its own type of backup software, or you can use a third-party backup program. (Note that the MS-DOS Backup utility doesn't support a tape drive.)

The advantage of using a tape drive is that you can back up without having to manually swap disks—which is a pain in the elbow no matter how fast the backup program is. Speed-wise, tape backups are relatively slow, so it helps if you can schedule them for a time when you're not using the computer; after hours or in the middle of the night is best.

As with disk backup sets, you also need to manage your tape backup cassettes. Be sure that you properly label the tapes and use appropriate-size cassettes for each type of backup. For very large hard-disk drives, this might present a problem; always get large cassettes for a full backup.

Although initially more expensive than using floppy disks, tape backups are far more convenient. For large computer systems, file services, and office environments where backups are important, consider getting a tape drive. (Since each system is specific, I won't go into detail here.)

What to Look for in Third-Party Backup Programs

The MS-DOS Backup utility is slow and inefficient, but you can't beat its price. If you have the money to spend and feel that a fast, efficient backup is more what you need, you can select from one of the several third-party backup programs. Here's what to look for.

Speed

All of these programs are fast, yet they will make millisecond comparisons with each other to determine who is top dog. That's really a moot point. More important than speed is their reliability, capacity, performance, and so on.

Capacity

This refers to how much information these programs can store on a disk. Using nonstandard disk formats, some third-party backup programs can squeeze a few extra kilobytes out of each floppy disk. Using data compression, they can pack even more data onto a single disk, which helps to cut down the number of disks needed, as well as the amount of time the backup requires.

Performance

Overall performance reflects a combination of speed and capacity, as well as how skillfully the program can handle glitched disks and other unusual circumstances. Also check the program's ability to restore backed-up files. While the backup process might be fast, the restore process might be agonizingly slow.

Flexibility

How much can you configure the program? Can it do a work-directory–only backup? Can it be run from a batch file? Does it have its own macro language? Can it talk to a tape drive? Chalk up bonus points if it meets any of these criteria.

Price

You pay for what you get. Most third-party backup programs sell for more than $100. You can figure that the price is worth it if you can make up the savings in time gained and disks used. I recommend going the third-party route if you're serious about backing up your files.

Keeping Your Emergency Boot Disk Updated

Every time you back up, be sure you copy any backup logs to your Emergency Boot Disk or to a special Backup/Recovery Disk. Remember, these important files must be kept safe in case your hard drive ever goes bananas. If you're running your backup from a batch file, include something like the following at the end of that batch file:

```
...
rem backup is done here
rem copy backup logs to the backup/recovery disk
echo Insert the Backup/Recovery Disk into drive A
pause
rem delete old log files (customize this command)
del a:*.log > nul
rem copy new log files (this one, too)
copy *.log a: > nul
echo Backup/Recovery Disk updated
:end
```

CARING FOR YOUR HARDWARE

Preventive medicine involves more than software. Your hardware deserves equal care. You don't need a screwdriver or any technical knowledge. A wee bit of cleaning now and then will make your computer last a little longer and give you less trouble.

Being Computer Friendly

So much emphasis is put on a computer being user-friendly that we forget the two-way street of friendship Miss Bradshaw taught us in second grade.

Give Mr. PC the Proper Supplies

Use the correct equipment with your PC: the proper disks, paper for the printer, ribbons, toner, and so on. Don't skimp on quality, and never use low-grade stuff that can fool the computer into thinking it's high-grade stuff. Don't alter or "punch" disks to magically make them higher capacity. This doesn't work.

Keep Mr. PC in a Well-Ventilated Area

PCs need to breathe. That noise you hear when a computer is turned on is its fan. The fan is actually part of the power supply and is designed to draw air in from the front of the system, over the hot electronic components, and blow it out the back. The PC needs to have all its breathing holes on both the front and back of the computer open and unobstructed.

Keep Mr. PC Away from Mr. Sun

Putting a computer in the sun only heats it up. A PC that gets too hot will turn itself off or behave in other unpredictable yet predictably bad ways.

Keep Mr. PC Away from Windows

For some reason, people like to put their computers next to windows. (Maybe that's where Bill Gates got the idea....) Criminals pick up on this, and the "smash-and-grab" becomes one of the most common methods of computer theft.

Spring Cleaning

Here are some things you can do every so often to keep your PC's hardware in tip-top shape. In most cases, you can keep the computer turned on while you're cleaning. However, for cleaning the keyboard or laser printer, I recommend turning everything off before you begin.

Cleaning the Keyboard

Wheel out your vacuum and attach that drapery-cleaning doohickey—you know, the one that looks like an aardvark's snout. Jab a straw into the narrow end of the attachment and anchor it with masking tape or duct tape. (Do this to the vacuum cleaner—not the aardvark.)

Seal the end of the drapery cleaner so that all the air travels through the straw. Then use that device to clean out the crud in your keyboard. (Similar tools are available from mail-order outlets, but they cost much more and don't give you that satisfying "I've done it myself" feeling.)

If you don't have a vacuum, you can clean your keyboard by popping off the key caps. I'm serious; you can do this. On most keyboards, the keycaps all pop off, although be careful to look for any gaskets, washers, or tiny springs that might come off with the caps. (If any do, this cleaning method might not be a good idea.) After the key caps are off, spray some 409 or Fantastik on a cloth and wipe out the keyboard. Have fun putting the caps back on in the right order!

Then there's the school of thought that says, "Give the keyboard a bath." Basically, you turn off the computer (which is a good idea anyway), unplug the keyboard, and then bathe it in some solution. This loosens all the filth, food remains, and (ugh) hair in the keyboard.

Why bother with all this? Because stuff in the keyboard can wedge itself between a key cap and the sensing mechanism in the keyboard, which might lead you to think a key is broken. (Keys on some keyboards contain small magnets which, when close enough to a sensor, tell the keyboard's brain that something is pressing that key.) In fact, I have even simply thumped my keyboard a few times to loosen the junk that gets stuck in it.

Cleaning Your Monitor

Every night the Pixel Fairy descends from the null device and deposits pixel dust on your screen. It's magic! To remove that thin layer of film, squirt some window cleaner or vinegar on a towel and gently wipe your monitor. Don't spray anything directly on the monitor; spray it on the towel first. Otherwise you risk getting cleaner on the innards of your monitor—not a good idea.

Blowing Air at the Subject

Believe it or not, you can visit just about any electronics store and buy a can of air. Use that can of pressurized air to blow the dust out of some parts of your computer, such as paper fragments from your printer.

You can also use the pressurized air to clean out the vents on your computer, especially those little holes on the front of your hard-disk drive. However, I recommend using the vacuum-cleaner attachment (described earlier) to *suck* the dust out instead of blowing it around inside the computer. Dust build-up can really shorten the life of electronic components. Too much dust in your PC's vents can lead to poor air circulation and overheating.

Cleaning the Printer

To clean a dot-matrix printer, you can use a can of air to blow out bits of paper. You can also use some isopropyl alcohol on a rag to clean the paper platen. (You might first have to remove the platen from the printer, which often requires taking the printer apart.)

Never use a can of air with laser printers; you should never blow anything into them. Instead, use a slightly damp cloth to gently wipe up the paper dust inside. This only needs to be done every few months, usually when you change the toner cartridge. For other general cleaning hints, follow the directions that come with the cartridge.

It's also best to change your printer's ribbon or toner cartridge frequently. Don't wait for a ribbon to become threadbare or your laser printer's image to go streaky before investing in a new ribbon or toner cartridge.

Caution! Klutz at Work

Simply being careful is a big part of prevention. Here are some things you can do to avoid damaging your computer while you work:

Watch Where You Put Your Pop

One common computer peripheral that isn't connected to the case by a cable is a cup of coffee or a can of pop. Be careful! Don't put your coffee or pop between the phone and your PC, between the mouse and the keyboard, or any place else where it could get knocked over and glup into the works.

Walking over Cables Is Not an Olympic Event

Route your cables so that no one will trip over them. You can always tape long cables to the carpet if necessary, or buy one of those floor-cable covers at an office supply store. Keep in mind that any cable left hanging by a walkway is like a baited hook to most people's fish feet.

Never Force Anything

Don't force a disk into a drive. Odds are either that the disk is oriented the wrong way or what you're jabbing the disk into is not your disk-drive slot. The same holds true for connectors. Just about everything inside and

outside a PC has a keyed type of connector; it can attach only one way. If
it doesn't fit, don't force it; reorient the connector and try again.

Increasing the Life Span of Your PC

In addition to all the other friendly hints offered here, you can increase the
life span of your PC by not turning it on and off each day. The worst case
is when you turn your computer on and off *several* times a day. The
theory goes that turning the PC on and off weakens the solder joints
due to the changing temperatures. That will make them brittle over time
and eventually crack them, leading to system failure.

Is it okay to leave your PC on all the time? Sure, providing you turn off
the monitor or use a "screen-dimming" program. That prevents the
dreaded *phosphor burn-in*, an image retained on the monitor even when
the monitor is turned off. (Thousands of early PCs had permanent etchings
of Lotus 1-2-3 on the screen.)

It's said that you subtract one day from your PC's life every time you
switch it off. My advice is to leave your system on all the time, turning
it off only when you'll be away for longer than a weekend. Be sure that
the computer room doesn't get too hot, and by all means, don't put a dust
cover on a PC that's turned on all the time.

SUMMARY

Preventive maintenance involves those simple chores you can do now to
avert disaster later. It involves protecting vital files against accidental deletion or damage, using MS-DOS tools such as the Mirror utility to keep
records of vital areas on disk, and backing up your data. You can remedy
nearly any situation if you have a backup disk handy.

For longer computing life and a happy PC, you should apply some tender
care to your hardware. True, these beasts can be robust. But with a little
extra attention, you can make them last longer—and look more present-
able (especially when being taunted by those newer, fancier computers
across the room).

Chapter 7

Solving Hardware Problems

It's best to take a systematic approach to tackling PC hardware problems. Rarely is any major surgery involved; most of the time, problems can be resolved with no loss of data and a minimum of hassle. Even the worst-case scenario has two simple solutions: Take the machine to a professional for repair or replace the defective part yourself.

Your computer is a collection of many individual components, each of which tries to work harmoniously with the others. To assist you in hunting down and solving hardware problems, this chapter describes the art of finding out which component is misbehaving and then deciding how to deal with the situation: whether to fix or repair what's wrong, or flat out replace it. If you opt to replace the malfunctioning part yourself, this chapter helps you by discussing strategies for buying computer components, including hints on shopping through the mail.

IS IT A HARDWARE PROBLEM?

The first step is to be certain that it's a hardware problem you're faced with. This is sometimes as obvious as seeing blue smoke rising from a PC when the power supply blows. (I'm not kidding here; from personal experience I *know* it's blue smoke.) Less obvious are problems with the keyboard, monitor, or a disk drive that might or might not be hardware-related. You need to learn how to spot the difference between hardware and software problems.

The best way to tell the origin of a problem is to check whether it's consistent across all your applications. If the problem creeps up only with certain programs or only in some environments, then it's probably a software problem. Universal problems and problems involving specific disks are hardware-related. (For more information about software problems, refer to Chapter 11.)

When you suspect a hardware problem, first review your current situation. Ask yourself the following questions.

Any Recent Software Changes?

Did you install anything new recently, specifically device drivers in your CONFIG.SYS file? Have you recently changed something in your CONFIG.SYS file, such as an option to an existing device driver, or did you delete something? For example, accidentally changing the Buffers configuration command to a value less than 10 (an inadvertent press of the Delete key can do this) can make your hard drive seem to operate in slow motion. Other mistakes might not be so subtle; due to a change in a memory device driver, I once had both floppy-disk drives assume they could format only 360-KB disks. Weird, yes. Hardware problem, no.

Software changes might also include modifications to existing programs. Unlike changes to CONFIG.SYS or AUTOEXEC.BAT, however, most programs don't have complete control over your computer. Programs like Microsoft Windows do, however, so be careful what you do to them, especially to Windows INI (initialization) files.

Any Recent Additions to the System?

Adding hardware or upgrading your hardware can affect your system. For example, upgrading to a VGA color system is good news. But remember to update or reinstall all your software to let it know about the new hardware or you'll have bad news. The same goes for new printers and printer drivers. Also be sure to properly configure your software for network operations and for using networked peripherals.

Is It a Speed Problem?

Most PCs have two speed modes: "turbo," or fast; and "compatible," or slow. You can change the speed with a special key combination or by pressing a button on the PC's front panel. The speed can also be changed by wayward programs that might not know they're stepping on some secret internal speed-switching location. If you notice your PC suddenly getting slower, try to switch it into turbo mode. If this works, review the programs you've just run to see if any are inadvertently changing your PC's speed.

Another problem exists with some dual-speed systems that aren't well designed. Frequent hard-drive errors or malfunctioning peripherals might be related to running the computer at fast speed. (This is a typical problem with some low-end PCs.) To verify that it's a speed problem, run the system in slow mode for a while. If the problem goes away, your system has a design flaw. Unfortunately, this problem can be fixed only by running your system in slow mode.

Has the PC Been Moved?

Moving a PC isn't a dangerous thing. In fact, most computers run during and after an earthquake. Mine did. The spinning hard disk acts as a gyroscope and keeps itself stable. (It's the power outage after the earthquake that causes the most damage.) However, even sliding a computer across the desktop can jostle some cables or loosen something that wasn't properly tightened in the first place.

Checking for loose items inside a PC is best done by someone familiar with the insides of a computer. I don't recommend hunting for loose cables or components if you've never opened a PC's case.

Are Cables Being Unreasonably Stretched?

Some intermittent problems with keyboards, monitors, and printers can occur because of your desktop arrangement. Some users stretch cables to their limits to make some sort of design statement. Eventually, a cable can pull loose—not all the way, but enough so it isn't obvious a full connection isn't being made. The solution: Don't stretch your cables.

What About the PC's Environment?

Where is the computer located? Is it beneath a window where it can heat up? What about the air circulation? Does the computer have room to breathe? Heat can stop a computer dead. Computers become unreliable and frequently switch themselves off if they are not kept cool.

Standard operating temperature for a computer should never rise above 80 degrees. If the computer overheats, you might have a hardware problem, but nothing an air conditioner or fan wouldn't help.

If you have a problem and it's hardware-related, keep reading. Otherwise, refer to Chapter 11 for additional help.

PROBLEM HUNTING

After determining that the problem is with the hardware, your job is to isolate the problem. The best way to proceed is to follow the boot process, starting with the power supply. Then work your way outward from the computer to its peripherals. During this process, if you discover that something needs to be repaired or replaced, refer to the section titled "Repairing Versus Replacing," later in this chapter.

To test your hardware, follow these steps.

Check the Power Supply

If you flip on the power switch and nothing happens, you have a power-supply problem. It could start at the wall: The power could be out, a fuse might be blown, or you might be in a "brownout" situation, where the power is on but too low to operate the computer. Or the problem could be the power cord. Check that it's plugged into both the wall and the computer. If the cord is plugged in, the problem is with the power supply in the computer. The power supply can be easily replaced and, thanks to its design, when a power supply goes bad, it usually doesn't damage the rest of the computer.

Power-On Self Test

If the power supply is okay, the computer will "come to life." The first thing every PC does is a *power-on self test*, or *POST*. The computer performs a battery of diagnostic tests on itself, ensuring that everything is performing properly. Most of the tests merely take inventory, happening quickly. The memory test takes the longest. Some PCs show the memory test on the screen as a RAM count, others just sit and hum.

The POST tests the items listed in Table 7-1, usually in the order of the table. Before the monitor is tested, POST errors will cause your system to beep. After the monitor is tested, the computer displays any errors as the numbers shown in Table 7-1 below. Those numbers are the traditional IBM numbers; newer systems may offer simple text messages as well. Some devices, such as video cards and network adapters, may have their own POSTs in addition to the PC's POST.

For example, a common boo-boo is caused by a missing or unplugged keyboard. In this case, your PC will start and display the error message 301. To fix the problem, turn off the system, plug in the keyboard, and start again. (On some systems that have text messages, this problem can cause a comical error message to appear: *Keyboard missing: Press any key to continue.*)

Memory errors result in 201 error messages, as well as the dreaded *Parity error* message. These errors are the hardest to locate, and they usually involve hunting for a rotten chip—which can take hours. Running diagnostic utilities, discussed in the next section, is a good step to take when you have a bad chip in your PC.

TABLE 7-1. THE POST INVENTORY AND ERROR LIST

Item Tested	Possible POST Error Messages
Power supply	No beep, long beep, or short beeps
Motherboard	Long beep, short beep
Speaker	No beep (obviously)
Video system	Long beep plus two or three short beeps, or two short beeps
Motherboard	101
Memory	201
Keyboard	301
Video	401, 501, 2401, 2501, 7401
Floppy drive	601
Math coprocessor	701
Printer port	901 or 1001
Serial port	1101 or 1201
Hard drive	1701 or 10401
Network card	3001 or 3101

The heart-stopping 1701 (or 10401) error message occurs when there's trouble with the hard-disk drive. Boot with your Emergency Boot Disk, and then read Chapter 8.

For other POST errors, refer to your system's manual or run the diagnostic disk that came with your computer (discussed in the next section). Most PCs survive the POST, so if you are still hunting for a hardware problem, keep looking.

Check the CMOS Memory

The CMOS, or battery backed-up RAM, contains information about a PC's configuration. Nearly all 80286 and later PCs have CMOS memory, which is accessed by running a special Setup program or by pressing a special key combination. If the CMOS goes bad or if the battery dies, your computer will lose track of things like memory installed, the hard-disk drive, the date and time, and so on.

If the POST detects any discrepancies between what's inside your PC and what the CMOS claims you have, an error message appears. You're usually given the chance to examine or change the CMOS setup immediately. This is when it pays to have a copy of the contents of your CMOS memory, as described in Chapter 1 (also see Appendix A). Compare that information with what CMOS is reporting, and then adjust any differences.

Note: If you've just upgraded memory or added a hard-disk drive, the CMOS error message always appears. This is how you inform the PC about the new memory, hard-disk drive, or other device. Make adjustments accordingly, and then reset.

If CMOS consistently reports hardware problems that don't exist, such as missing memory, missing hard-disk drives, inaccurate date or time—and when fixing these components doesn't help—the CMOS memory might be bad or it might need a new battery. Refer to your PC's manual for information on replacing the CMOS battery. (This problem usually occurs after your PC's fourth birthday.)

Check the Monitor, Printer, and Other Peripherals

Check the system's peripheral items. Be sure everything is properly connected, plugged in, switched on, and ready to run.

Monitors have brightness switches that, when turned down, give the illusion that the monitor isn't working. Other knobs can slide the image to one side or the other of the screen, or adjust the horizontal or vertical size of the image. Adjust these knobs before you assume the monitor is broken.

Printers must be plugged in *and* be online or selected before they can print. In addition, printers must be in the proper mode for printing. You select the print mode when you set up your software; always install the proper printer configuration. If you don't, it might appear as though your printer is broken, when in reality it simply can't understand the instructions the PC is sending it.

Check keyboards and other peripherals for proper connections, power switches, and so forth. Some keyboards have an "XT-AT" switch, which configures them for operation with an 8088/8086 or 80286-level system. Be sure the switch is set properly for your PC.

Your mouse works best on a flat, textured surface. Check to be sure no one has stolen your mouse ball (a common prank).

Check Internal Switches and Cables

Finally, you might need to check internal switches, jumpers, and cable connections inside your PC. These things can wiggle loose, especially if you've just upgraded your hardware; putting the lid back on a PC has been known to pull out hard-disk drive cables. Always be careful when you're inside a PC. If you're willing to venture in there, take the extra time needed to double-check cable connections and to verify that all switches, jumpers, and whatnot are properly installed.

What Breaks First?

Narrowing down the search for a hardware problem is easier if you know what's likely to break first. It's like being an auto mechanic who can tell exactly what's wrong with a car simply by listening to it.

After the first few weeks of operation, electronic components in a PC are eternally stable. Only design flaws, power outages, or disasters can damage the electronic parts of a PC. This puts the mechanical, or moving, parts at the top of the breakdown list. And the first item on that list is the constantly spinning disk drive.

Floppy-disk drives can experience problems from wear and use. This is not a serious issue in a computer with a hard-disk drive; floppy-disk drives can easily be replaced. Hard-disk drives, on the other hand, are central to the system's operation. As long as you frequently back up and safeguard your system, you can recover from a hard-disk drive disaster.

Telltale signs of hard-disk drive wear are bad sectors, read/write errors, and media errors. These occur more frequently as the hard-disk drive ages. In fact, if a four-year-old hard-disk drive starts reporting more and more errors, it's simply nature's way of telling you that a new hard-disk drive is needed. These errors can sometimes be fixed on newer hard-disk drives by revitalizing the disk format. (See Chapter 10 for more information.)

The keyboard, being mechanical, is also susceptible to damage. Keys can get stuck, stop functioning, or break off—depending on how violent a typist you are. Repairing a keyboard or replacing key caps is a common solution to keyboard problems. But one thing few users know is that the keyboard has a computer all its own; inside the keyboard is a microprocessor which translates your keystrokes into signals. These signals are sent along the keyboard cable, a special type of serial cable, to the computer, where the keystrokes are interpreted.

If you've narrowed down your hardware problem to one of the mechanical devices in your PC, you're halfway home. Further troubleshooting, poking, and prodding is all you need to confirm that something needs to be repaired or replaced.

Simple Things You Can Do

Before putting your PC under the knife, or seriously looking at mail order replacement parts, consider the following simple things you can do to remedy the situation.

Check the Cable Connections

This is one of the axioms of hardware troubleshooting, repeated many times in computer folklore and in this book. Check all your cables, including internal ones for items such as disk drives. Incidentally, internal cables in a PC are usually notched or "keyed" in a way such that they cannot be plugged in backward.

Run Your Diagnostics Disk

Most PCs come with a diagnostics disk. Boot the system with that disk and run through the utilities on it. This is most useful when you're hunting down memory problems; depending on the sophistication of the utility, you might be given an exact location for a bad RAM chip.

Third-party peripherals might also come with diagnostic disks. If your video card, printer, memory cards, scanner, mouse, and so on each has its own diagnostic disk, use it.

Swap Out Bad or Questionable Parts

A quick way to test questionable equipment is to "swap out" that equipment. For example, swap keyboards with another PC if you suspect your keyboard is causing problems. Be sure both systems are turned off before you unplug the keyboards. Then turn on the computers and see how each behaves. If the "bad" keyboard works on the second computer—but the second computer's good keyboard suddenly malfunctions—you might have a motherboard problem, a problem with the keyboard's connector, or a stretched cable.

It's easy to swap out keyboards, monitors, and printers. You can also swap out floppy-disk drives and power supplies, although that involves a higher degree of technical proficiency. It may be easier simply to replace floppy-disk drives and power supplies.

Check the Interrupts

Interrupts often cause hardware distress. The problem appears only after you've added a fancy new peripheral to your system, such as a scanner, mouse, CD-ROM drive, or sound card. Interrupt problems can be resolved, usually without having to sacrifice anything in your computer. Interrupt problems are addressed in detail starting in the next section.

If you try all of these simple things and nothing seems to help, you must make a major decision: Do you take the hardware to the repair shop, or do you buy a replacement? To help you decide what to do, read the section "Repairing Versus Replacing," at the end of this chapter.

INTERRUPTS: THE BANE OF EXISTENCE

Interrupts are quirky little things—like heartbeats—that every computer has and cannot live without. They are quirky because the average computer, based on the original IBM equipment, has only so many interrupts to go around. Further, just about every piece of hardware and its cousins are anxious to grab an interrupt in a PC. This smells like trouble.

What Are Interrupts?

Interrupts are just what the name implies: interruptions. People get them every day—TV commercials, stoplights, and spouses. The telephone is an interrupt: No matter what you're doing, you stop to answer the phone. Computers work the same way.

A computer interrupt is tied to some hardware device. For example, every PC has a timer tick interrupt. It's the PC's heartbeat, going off some 18.5 times a second. Every .054 or so seconds, your computer stops what it's doing so that the clock can go "tick"; .054 seconds later, the clock interrupt stops everything and goes "tock." This goes on constantly in all PCs.

Consider the typical serial port, also hooked to an interrupt. Suppose a character comes wandering in through your modem. The modem sends that character to the serial port, and the serial port generates an interrupt. That interrupt travels through the serial hardware to your computer's microprocessor, and everything is put on hold. The microprocessor then picks up the character from a preassigned location. After the microprocessor finishes processing the character, it returns to whatever it was doing before the character appeared.

Interrupts are also handy. Without them, the computer would have to manually check on everything all the time. With interrupts, the microprocessor handles certain events automatically: writing to the disk drive, reading from the keyboard, updating the internal clock, monitoring the mouse, and so on. Thanks to interrupts, these jobs are handled as they occur.

Interrupts in a Typical PC

The design of a typical PC supports 16 hardware interrupts, or Interrupt Request Channels (IRQs). These are direct lines of communication from hardware add-ons, usually cards you plug into the expansion slots, and the microprocessor. Table 7-2 lists all 16 interrupts. However, because there are only 16 interrupts, interrupts and interrupt conflicts can lead to much gnashing of teeth.

Having 16 interrupts seems like a lot, but almost all of them are used by something. Old 8088/8086-based systems have even fewer interrupts available: only the first 7 interrupts listed in Table 7-2. Interrupt 2 was used for a hard disk, network adapters, clock, or joystick, and interrupt 5 was used for a hard-disk drive, printer, or mouse.

The list of interrupts can be rather deceiving; it almost looks like every possible piece of hardware is covered. But what about network adapters?

TABLE 7-2. THE 16 INTERRUPTS IN A PC

IRQ	Used By
0	Timer tick
1	Keyboard
2	Secondary interrupts (8 through 15)
3	Second and fourth serial ports (COM2, COM4)
4	First and third serial ports (COM1, COM3)
5	Second printer port (LPT2); reserved on PS/2 computers
6	Floppy-disk drive
7	Printer port (LPT1)
8	Real-time clock
9	Redirected from IRQ 2
10	Reserved
11	Reserved
12	Mouse; reserved on PC/AT computers
13	Math coprocessor
14	Hard-disk drive
15	Reserved

Or the popular sound-generation hardware many users love? What if you add a SCSI controller to your system? Where would its interrupts go?

Problems arise when two interrupts conflict. No one interrupt can be "shared" by two pieces of hardware. For example, you think you have installation down pat, but when you turn on your PC, you discover your new sound card *and* your mouse no longer work. Finding a solution to this problem means resolving the interrupt conflict between those two devices.

Resolving Interrupt Conflicts

Resolving interrupt conflicts works along the same lines as avoiding them: Know what you have in your computer and take advantage of unused interrupt lines whenever possible. Usually, you can safely "steal" the interrupts used by COM2 and LPT2. If you don't have a second serial or printer port on your system, consider using interrupts 3 or 5 for other devices. This sounds easy, but in practice choosing interrupts can be difficult.

The number of devices that require interrupts is staggering. For starters, consider CD-ROM drives, internal modems, pointing devices, network adapters, scanners, and sound cards. They all need interrupts. No PC can handle all of them, so you must be selective. Thankfully, most hardware add-ons that use interrupts let you select which interrupt to use. Before you plug the card into an expansion slot, you're directed to set an interrupt line by moving a small plastic tab, or *jumper*, to the proper position. The add-on device's manual usually offers a few suggestions that help resolve interrupt conflicts.

For example, your bus mouse card lets you select interrupts 2, 3, 4, or 5. The manual lists interrupts you *should not* use, which helps you narrow down your options. For adding other cards, the interrupt-resolution grid shown in Table 7-3 can aid your decision.

Note: PS/2 systems, and other computers with Micro Channel or similar architecture, can use software to set interrupts. In some cases, conflict resolutions might be made automatically by the expansion card. If the card isn't that smart, you select an interrupt in the same way you do for non-PS/2 expansion cards.

In Table 7-3, mark the interrupts used on your PC. Some interrupts are always assigned to specific items: The timer uses interrupt 0; the keyboard uses interrupt 1; the real-time clock uses interrupt 8; and a math co-processor always uses interrupt 13. Note which interrupts other devices in your system (serial ports, hard-disk drives, floppy-disk drives, and so on) use. If the device's manual doesn't help you, use Table 7-2 as an example.

When you add hardware to your system, use Table 7-3 to assign available interrupts to it. The Xs in Table 7-3 indicate interrupts that are not available. Assigning interrupts can get tricky: If you run out of interrupts, you're out. The PC's design doesn't give you any more. You'll either have to sacrifice something or resort to a work-around solution.

An example of a work-around solution is an external modem. It operates off a serial port, which already has its own interrupt. This saves one

TABLE 7-3. THE INTERRUPT RESOLUTION GRID

Device	0	1	2	3	4	5	6	7	8	9	10	11	12	13	14	15
Timer	X															
Keyboard		X														
COM2, COM4																
COM1, COM3																
LPT2																
Floppy-disk drive																
LPT1																
Real-time clock									X							
Math coprocessor														X		
Hard-disk drive																
Mouse																
Network adapter																
Sound card																
CD-ROM																
Scanner																

interrupt. Using a serial mouse also saves an interrupt that would otherwise be used by the mouse card.

Or suppose you want to attach both a scanner and a CD-ROM drive to your computer. Instead of wrestling with each, consider installing a SCSI (pronounced "scuzzy") interface. This will use an interrupt, but it saves any interrupts required by the devices you attach to the SCSI port.

Then you can get really sneaky: Some laptop network adapters work off of the printer port. True, these adapters are expensive and not as fast as your standard network card, but they use the printer port's interrupt. Another network solution is to sacrifice LPT2—or even LPT1—in favor of a network adapter and then use the network printer. This eliminates local printing, but it gives you back an interrupt that you can use for a sound card, modem, or mouse.

The best part about juggling interrupts (as if there were a best part!) is that after you do it—and get it to work—you'll never need to mess with interrupts again. Okay, if you buy another device that requires an interrupt, your juggling act resumes. But unlike software tuning and performance adjustment, working out interrupt conflicts is a once-a-year event—at the most.

Other Conflicts to Resolve:
I/O Port Address and Memory

In addition to interrupt conflicts, hardware adapters can have I/O port address conflicts. These are specific lines into the microprocessor over which two or more devices might skirmish.

A common battle waged in early PCs was over the first parallel printer port, LPT1. Some PCs came with the printer port, LPT1, on its own card. When a graphics adapter, such as the CGA or Hercules, was added, it also came with a printer port, LPT1. The PC resolved this conflict by shutting down both printer ports.

Today you can resolve most I/O port address conflicts by moving jumpers or configuring hardware so that no two devices share the same I/O ports or memory. In the case of two LPT1 ports, you simply assign one as LPT2 or disable one of the two.

Table 7-4 lists the I/O port addresses of popular devices in PCs. The devices listed have priority over those port addresses. Any other devices you add should use their own unique addresses, or they can "borrow" the address of some device your system doesn't have. Beware of borrowing, however; at some distant time you might add that certain device, which means you must repeat the entire process.

If a device uses an I/O port address between some of the listed addresses, that's okay. For example, some ARCNET network adapters squeeze themselves between the serial port addresses shown in Table 7-4. As long as that space isn't used by something else, it's okay.

Further tussles are possible with memory address conflicts. Chapter 6 mentioned a conflict with the EMS page frame. The page frame must be a contiguous 64 KB of upper memory. If you have adapter cards using small chunks of memory, there might not be a block large enough for the page

TABLE 7-4. I/O ADDRESSES FOR VARIOUS DEVICES IN A PC

Port Address (Hex)	Hardware
040–05F	Timer
060	Keyboard
070–07F	Real-time clock
0F8–0FF	Math coprocessor
1F0–1F8	Hard-disk drive
200–20F	Joystick
278–27F	Second printer port (LPT2)
2E0–2E7	Fourth serial port (COM4)
2E8–2EF	Third serial port (COM3)
2F8–2FF	Second serial port (COM2)
360–363	Network
368–36B	Network
378–37F	Printer port (LPT1)
3F0–3F7	Floppy-disk drive
3F8–3FF	First serial port (COM1)

frame. Other conflicts can come from nonstandard hard-drive controllers or with video BIOS not located in the traditional spot.

Figure 7-1 shows an upper memory map. Fill in this upper memory map with the ROM and RAM locations used in your computer. The locations are listed in *hexadecimal*, or base 16. That's a programmer's counting base, but it's also what every hardware manufacturer uses when plotting locations in upper memory. We must live with it.

Each bank of upper memory is equal to 64 KB and each is labeled with a letter, A through F. Further, each bank is divided into 16-KB chunks. These pan out to hexadecimal values 400, 800, and C00, as shown in Figure 7-1. Additional tick marks are provided at the 8-KB address boundaries: 200, 600, A00, and E00, although they are not marked in Figure 7-1.

Feel free to fill in some of the more common memory locations in all PCs:

Device	Address Range
Monochrome video memory	B000 to B200
CGA video memory	B800 to BC00
EGA video memory	A000 to B000, and B800 to C000
VGA video memory	A000 to B000, and B800 to C000
EGA video BIOS	C000 to C400
VGA video BIOS	C000 to C800
Hard-disk controller	C800 to CC00
System BIOS	F000 to end of memory

If you know that a device you've just installed, such as an EMS card's page frame, is in another location, shade it in the map as well. Doing this will assist you with other adapter cards that occupy space in upper memory; refer to the chart and assign unused memory to the adapter card. Remember to shade in and label the adapter card in Figure 7-1.

As with juggling interrupts and I/O port addresses, you select the memory location for hardware by setting jumpers or tiny switches on the card itself. With some cards, you might assign memory locations using a setup program or with a device driver in CONFIG.SYS. Be sure to set the memory location so that it doesn't conflict with areas of memory used by other adapters.

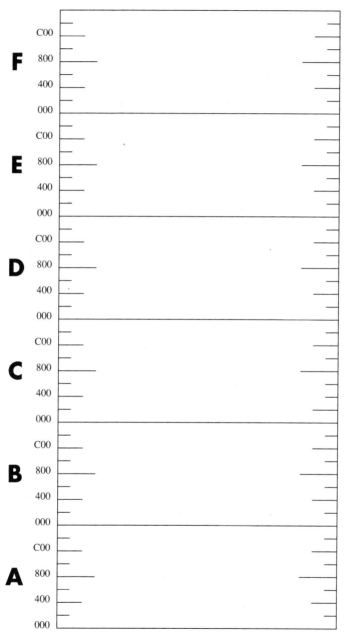

Figure 7-1. *The upper memory map.*

REPAIRING VERSUS REPLACING

When a problem can't be resolved and you're fairly certain you know which piece of hardware is defective, you have two choices: You can take your PC in for repairs, or you can replace the defective part yourself.

Unless you're an electronics wiz, don't ever figure on repairing something yourself. Replacing, however, is something anyone can do. The PC is a modular device; you can replace parts using nothing more than a screwdriver and a few moments of your time. However, if tinkering with your PC bothers you, the repair doctor can replace or upgrade parts for you, often for only a nominal fee.

What's Possible and What's Not

Before deciding whether to have something repaired or replaced, you must know what's reasonable to repair. Nearly everything inside a PC can be repaired by a competent PC technician. However, the merits of fixing a floppy-disk drive at the cost of $75 an hour when new drives cost about $50 are questionable. For all but a few components, replacing them with faster and better parts is cheaper than fixing old ones.

The first thing to check is the warranty. If your PC or that specific part is under warranty, contact your dealer about getting a replacement.

When the PC is no longer under warranty, it's time to call the doctor. Describe the problem and ask what they charge for an estimate. (It's usually $15 or $25.) Also ask which parts of the PC you need to bring in and be sure to ask the technician whether any cables are needed. Then take in your PC for an estimate only. Have the technician phone you with the results.

Ask for an estimate of the repair costs. For repairs, most places charge about $75 per hour, plus parts. If the estimate sounds reasonable, go for it. Expect your PC back in three to five days, although if you pay through the nose you can get it back sooner.

What can a PC doctor repair? Just about anything. But take my advice about repairing the following items:

Monitors

Monitors can be tweaked in much the same way as TVs. But the adjustments here are only cosmetic: a technician can straighten out and focus an image, but for heavy-duty repairs, buying a new monitor is usually cheaper. (Most reputable repair places will tell you that up front.)

Hard-Disk Drives

It's better to replace hard-disk drives than repair them. However, a technician can tell you whether the problem is with the drive itself or with the controller. In either case, it's still cheaper to buy a new drive or controller rather than repair the old one. However, if you need to recover data (you don't have a backup and the information on your hard-disk drive is important), many technicians will attempt to recover your data. There's a high success rate, but you might pay dearly for it.

Motherboards

Trouble with the motherboard, expansion cards, and other circuitry can be spotted only by competent technicians. If repairs are possible, go for it. It's possible to replace and upgrade motherboards, but doing so is usually more expensive than repairing them.

Printers

Never mess with the innards of your printer. Unless you plan to replace the entire printer, have the doctor fix it.

If what's ailing your computer is something other than the monitor, hard-disk drive, motherboard, or printer, consider buying a new part and installing it yourself.

Buying Replacement Parts

You can replace a defective, worn out, or aging piece of hardware in your computer with a similar item, or you can upgrade. To swap parts, you need to know the manufacturer's name and model number of the part. To get this information, you might have to open the PC to extract a power supply, disk drive, or expansion card.

If you upgrade, choose a better, faster piece of hardware, but keep in mind that it must still be compatible with your system. If you decide to replace something, read the following list of compatibility concerns. The list will help you ensure that the replacement or upgrade will match what you already have.

Monitors

A monitor is only one half of your video system. You also need a compatible video adapter. The new monitor must work with your video adapter. To upgrade a monitor, you must upgrade your video adapter as well.

Video Adapters

A video adapter must be compatible with your monitor. If you're upgrading to a color system from monochrome, you'll need both a color adapter and a monitor. If you're upgrading only the adapter, be sure the monitor will work with the upgraded adapter. Keep an eye out for the *scanning frequency*, and be sure that it matches your monitor.

Some video adapters come with printer ports. Check your system for existing printer ports that might conflict with the port on the video adapter.

Hard-Disk Drives

Hard-disk drives must be compatible with the hard-disk drive controller. One of these five types of controllers are used in most PCs: MFM, RLL, ESDI, IDE, and SCSI. For MFM and RLL controllers (found mostly in older PC/XTs), the replacement hard-disk drive must be of the same size and capacity as the original. Other controllers can handle larger and faster hard-disk drives.

Another issue with hard-disk drives, and with disk drives in general, is their *form factor*. This refers to the physical size of the drive. If you're replacing a large-format 5¼-inch drive with a smaller 3½-inch drive, be sure you get the proper mounting brackets. If you're replacing a small drive with a big one, be sure the new one will fit.

Hard-Disk Controllers

Hard-disk controllers must match the drives already in your system. If the controller doesn't match, or if there's even a subtle difference, you'll have to reformat your hard-disk drives. This is primarily of concern for MFM and RLL controllers. Other controllers can be replaced quite easily.

Power Supplies

Power supplies are "plug-in and replace," but you must be aware of the wattage. Replacing your power supply with a higher-wattage power supply is a good idea—for example, replacing a 150W with a 200W power supply. Watch the case size. Some generic power supplies are designed for the old-style PC/AT case; they're much too big for many of today's slimmer PCs.

Keyboards

Upgrading or replacing your keyboard is a snap. Some keyboards might work only with PC/XTs or PC/ATs; others might support both systems but have a tiny switch that sets up the keyboard one way or the other. Note that some older PCs might not be able to read the extended keys on the 101-key enhanced keyboard.

Memory Upgrades

Upgrading memory is always a good thing to do. Be sure to buy memory that matches your system's requirements. Those little black chips may all look the same, but they're not!

Buying Mail-Order Parts

You can opt to have a computer doctor or your dealer replace the defective part. If you're good with tinkering, however, you might want to buy the part via mail order and save a few dollars. It pays to shop around, but if you don't find any deals or are leery of replacing a part yourself, stick with a dealer. If you decide to buy mail-order parts, you'll soon find yourself scouring computer hardware ads like the one shown in Figure 7-2 on the next page. Tips for reading such an ad are provided below.

Monitors

Monitors vary in price based on their performance and image quality. Some ads list the monitor's *dot pitch*—the distance between individual pixels on the screen—in hundredths of a millimeter. The closer the dots, the finer the image; a dot pitch of .28 mm is ideal.

Other ways to describe a monitor include its bandwidth value in megahertz (MHz), interlacing, scan rate, and picture-tube size. Most of these are technical values, the specifics of which are important only when you

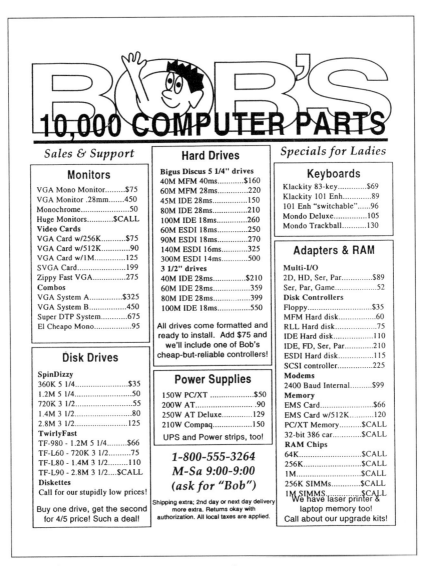

Figure 7-2. *Bob's 10,000 Computer Parts ad.*

compare them to your video card. As you can predict, larger monitors, such as presentation monitors or special monitors for desktop publishing, cost more.

I've purchased monochrome monitors through a mail-order house. For color monitors, I prefer buying one at a dealer where I can compare two or more side by side. If you want to really test a monitor, have the dealer run Microsoft Windows.

Floppy-Disk Drives

Floppy-disk drives are typically generic, although a few brand-name drives exist. The two things you're looking for are the size, 5¼-inch or 3½-inch, and the capacity. I'd avoid cheap drives.

Hard-Disk Drives

Hard-disk drives can be confusing things to order, primarily because of all the part numbers. (I know some hardcore computer nerds who refer to drives exclusively by number.) Check the drive for compatibility with your hard-disk controller. The ad in Figure 7-2 offers MFM, IDE, and ESDI drives. Check the size (in megabytes, the M values in Figure 7-2) offered. MFM and RLL drives must match the size of the drive you're replacing. Otherwise, more is better and more is expensive.

The speed of a drive is given in milliseconds (abbreviated as "ms" in Figure 7-2). The lower this value, the faster the drive, and the more money you pay. Try to avoid drives with ratings greater than 40 ms. A fast drive, 28 or 18 ms, is worth the price; it's an excellent way to speed up an old, sluggish computer without buying a faster model.

Finally, look for the physical drive size: 5¼ inches or 3½ inches. Try to match the drive you're replacing. If not, request some mounting brackets.

Power Supplies

Power supplies are easy to buy. Match the wattage with what you need: 150W is good for 8088/8086 systems; 200W and higher is recommended for PC/AT and later systems. Be sure the power supply's size matches your PC's case. Also, note that some systems, such as Compaq computers, require their own unique power supplies.

Keyboards

The most common PC keyboard is the 101-key enhanced keyboard. Generally speaking, the more a keyboard costs, the better its design and touch. Expect a spongy response from cheaper brands. Some of the fancier keyboards also offer special features, such as left-handed keyboards and built-in track-balls. If you have a PC/XT, remember to get a special PC/XT keyboard.

Adapters and RAM

Adapters are anything that plugs into an expansion slot in your PC. Multi-I/O cards are designed to expand the system, giving you more serial ports, printer ports, a joystick port, a clock, or additional memory. As mentioned earlier in this chapter, this is where you'll get PC interrupt headache, trying to make these devices compatible with any already in your system.

For video and hard-disk controllers, remember to buy a controller that matches your current monitor or hard-disk drive. I recommend buying a VGA video card that has at least 512 KB of RAM. SuperVGA cards are better, and more memory is better if you can afford it. Keep in mind that upgrading the memory on these cards isn't as easy as upgrading general memory; buy the memory now. When you pay more for a VGA card, you gain a bit more capability. However, beware of expensive models—they might offer features you'll never use.

Hard-disk controllers are sold by the type of drive they support: MFM, RLL, IDE, ESDI, and SCSI are the most popular. The IDE and ESDI drives are currently the most popular ones. Most controllers support two hard-disk drives in addition to two floppy-disk drives. Some controllers might also contain serial and printer ports; for example, the *IDE, FD, Ser, Par* card listed in Figure 7-2 is such a card: FD stands for floppy-disk drive, Ser for serial port, and Par for printer (parallel) port.

Memory is purchased by the "tube." You'll need to know the following: how much memory you'll need in kilobytes or megabytes; the size of the chips (256 KB, 1 MB, and so on); the quantity of chips; whether you need SIMMs; the speed of the chips in nanoseconds (ns); and any other special information described in the hardware manual.

Important Questions to Ask

In addition to buying the right part, here are some key questions to ask any mail-order vendor:

■ *Who supports the warranty?*

If the vendor does, great! If the warranty is passed off to the manu-facturer, be sure you get the support number.

■ *Does the vendor have phone support?*

Support from the mail-order vendor can range from nonexistent to a toll-free 800 line for technical questions. Be sure to ask.

■ *Are there any extra charges?*

Some places charge extra for using credit cards, or only for certain cards. Try to avoid any mail-order dealer who offers a discount for prepaid orders. That usually implies sending cash or a check. Don't bother.

■ *What about substitutions?*

Ask if the vendor substitutes items or ships refurbished items or "seconds." Don't accept any substitution unless you personally ap-prove it.

■ *How is it shipped?*

Shipping things through the mail isn't much of a problem. Most items arrive safe and sound. Ask if shipping is included. Also check to see if alternative forms of shipping (UPS, overnight, and so on) are available.

■ *What about the return policy?*

Everything from a mail-order vendor should be covered by a return policy. Most of the better dealers offer 30-day money-back guaran-tees. Verify how much of your money you get back, or whether some of it goes for "restocking fees" or "handling."

You should be able to return damaged or D.O.A. items with no ques-tions asked. Find out who pays for this shipping. Further, find out if the vendor fixes broken items or if you have to send a damaged part to the manufacturer.

Above all, use your best judgement. There are many mail-order houses to choose from. If you feel you're being treated rudely or the salesperson is condescending, call someone else.

Installing It Yourself

You don't always have to install new equipment yourself. A computer dealer or repair doctor can do it for you, often for as little as a $25 service fee—or sometimes for free if you buy the part there. Local computer gurus can do it as well. They usually advertise their services in local papers.

If you end up installing a part yourself, follow this advice: Be careful. Always turn off and unplug the PC before you open its case. Follow the installation instructions that came with the new part or read and follow the instructions in one of the many books available on the upgrading and repairing of PCs.

After you install the part, remember to test your new hardware. You may need to flip some switches, run your setup program and modify the CMOS memory, or juggle some interrupts. You might also have to update your CONFIG.SYS or your applications, letting them know about the replacement upgrade. In no time at all, your hardware problem is solved.

SUMMARY

Fixing hardware problems involves two steps. The first is to figure out what is broken, especially whether the problem is related to a specific piece of hardware. After that, you must decide between repairing the broken part or replacing it outright.

One of the most agonizing aspects of troubleshooting hardware problems is getting various hardware devices to work together inside the somewhat limited PC. This involves juggling interrupts, sorting them out to the right pieces of hardware in the proper order. Trial and error works best here.

Fortunately, most hardware problems are easily mended and you're back on your way quickly. For information about software problems, see Chapter 11. Now read on. The next chapter covers the scariest part of hardware failure—*The Big One*: failure of the hard-disk drive.

Chapter 8

When The Big One Hits

Not everything that goes wrong in a PC is "the big one." Sometimes problems are performance related; improving performance by defragmenting a hard disk or adding a cache solves the problem. Sometimes problems are hardware related; you can pinpoint problems by using the steps discussed in Chapter 7. Then you either repair or replace the defective part. But the worst nightmares, the problems that raise your blood pressure higher and faster than all the rest, are disk problems.

This chapter tells you how to deal with major hard-disk maladies. Disk problems are many, including accidentally losing files, deleting subdirectories, reformatting important disks, and general hard-drive trouble, yet not all of these problems spell disaster. This chapter discusses ways you can recover from these problems. And if you've followed the steps outlined earlier in this book, recovery will be even easier.

RESET RECOVERY

Most users don't consider resetting their computers to be a dangerous act. As long as resetting is done properly, pressing Ctrl+Alt+Delete or pressing a Reset button isn't anything to worry about. Resetting in panic situations or to quickly and improperly exit an application is another story.

The most common way uninformed users quit a program is by resetting. It's fast and easy, and it's a "common" command: Pressing Ctrl+Alt+ Delete stops the program, and in only a matter of seconds you're back at the MS-DOS prompt, ready to run another program. Some people are so used to this method that they consider it the acceptable way to use an MS-DOS computer. Wrong. Wrong. Wrong.

Always quit a program properly, exit to MS-DOS, and then run another program from the MS-DOS prompt, from your menu-based program, or from Windows.

There are times, however, when resetting from a program is necessary. MS-DOS programs aren't perfect, and sometimes they lock up. Further, it might not be obvious how to exit an application, and you might want to reset just to collect your wits. When you feel you've reached that point, follow these steps:

1. Press Ctrl+C, Ctrl+Break, the Esc key, or the program's Cancel key. These should be your first attempts to gracefully back out of a problematic situation.

   In Windows, you can press Ctrl+Esc to summon the Task Manager. From there, you can switch to another program, or you can remove a locked-up program by highlighting its name and choosing the End Task button.

2. If the computer behaves in an unusual way, you'll have to reset. For example, if the keyboard starts beeping, you've filled the type-ahead buffer and the keyboard is essentially deaf to your input. Press Ctrl+Alt+Delete. If that doesn't work, press your PC's Reset button. If your PC doesn't have a Reset button, turn off the power. Wait about a minute, and then turn the power back on.

3. After resetting, use the Chkdsk command to check for lost files. On computers where resetting is a matter of course, Chkdsk will find dozens of lost file clusters. (That's actually what makes those systems so sluggish after a while.) If you've reset in a panic, then Chkdsk might find a few file fragments. Use this command:

```
C> chkdsk /f
```

The /F switch alerts Chkdsk to convert any lost chains or allocation units into files. If any lost chains or allocation units are found, you'll see the following prompt:

```
Convert lost chains into files (Y/N)?
```

Press Y. Chkdsk converts the chains into files in the root directory. The files are named FILE*xxxx*.CHK, where *xxxx* is a four-digit number starting with 0000. Typically, the files contain nothing interesting. Even if they did, it's hard to determine what their original names were or to which application they belong; it's best to delete them all.

4. If you were running Windows, delete the Windows temporary files. Normally, Windows deletes these files when you exit properly. After resetting, however, you should manually delete them.

   Note: Do not manually remove temporary files from within Windows.

   All Windows temporary files start with a tilde (~). Use the following command to delete them all:

   ```
   C> del ~*.*
   ```

   Or you can insert the following line in your AUTOEXEC.BAT file:

   ```
   if exist ~*.* del ~*.* > nul
   ```

   This command first checks for Windows temporary files using the IF-EXIST test. If any temporary files are found, they're deleted with the Del command; any output is redirected to the NUL device.

5. Continue using your PC as you normally would.

   Other programs besides Windows might have created temporary or backup files. For example, you might have the "timed backup" option working in a few programs (which is always a good idea). When you start these programs, you might be alerted to the presence of the backup files. Do not delete these files! Look over any backup files and recover any data that might be in them.

Keep in mind that none of these steps are needed if you've reset from the MS-DOS prompt. For example, if you've reset to load a new device driver in CONFIG.SYS, there's no need to clean up files or to run Chkdsk.

UNDELETING FILES

One of the most foolish things users do is delete important files. It's too easy. Even if you're careful, you might find out you're in the wrong directory or on the wrong drive when you typed *del *.**. Thankfully, MS-DOS has an Undelete command that helps you recover freshly deleted files.

Although Undelete is handy, it's not an excuse for carelessness with the Del or Erase commands.

How Can a File Be "Undeleted"?

For many years, undeleting files was in the domain of third-party utilities. Quite a few programmers got rich off their wizardry at doing the impossible: reviving a file that MS-DOS had deleted. It was gone! Zapped out of existence. Yet certain utilities could resurrect it. How'd they do that?

The truth is, files are never really deleted by MS-DOS. Just as you don't kill someone by deleting their name from your address book, MS-DOS never destroys a file when you remove it with the Del or Erase commands. Getting it back involves only a wee bit of magic, but mostly a knowledge of how MS-DOS deletes—or doesn't delete—files in the first place.

To demonstrate this, format a new floppy disk—or QuickFormat an older disk. Don't give the disk a volume label. Enter the following:

```
C>format a:
```

You'll place two files on this disk, one of which you'll delete and then revive using Debug. This is a simple demonstration of a complex function—and it's not always foolproof, which is why a new disk is needed. After the disk is formatted, return to MS-DOS and create two small files:

```
C>copy con a:test1
this is a test
^Z
        1 file(s) copied
```

And:

```
C>copy con a:test2
this is another test
^Z
        1 file(s) copied
```

(Press F6 or Ctrl+Z to end input and create the file.)

Start Debug by entering *debug* at the MS-DOS prompt. Debug's friendly hyphen prompt greets you.

```
C>debug
```

In addition to looking at memory and creating (or debugging) small programs, you can use Debug to look at sectors on a disk. The sectors are loaded into memory, where you can work on them. Then, if you like, you can rewrite the sectors back to disk. (That's the dangerous part.)

Load the first several sectors from the floppy disk in drive A with the following Debug command:

```
-1 100 0 0 26
```

Note that the first character is an L—not a one. The next value is 100, the address at which the sectors will be loaded, followed by 0 for drive A, 0 for the first sector on the disk, and 26 for the total number of sectors (38 decimal). Remember that Debug uses hexadecimal numbers exclusively.

After your disk drive whirs for a few moments, the sectors will be loaded. There are four key items loaded: the boot sector, two copies of the file allocation table (FAT), and the root directory. These items are kept in various sectors, depending on the size of the disk.

Table 8-1 shows which sectors hold the boot sector, the FATs, and the root directory, depending on the size of your disk. It also shows the locations where those items are now located in memory according to Debug. You can use the D ("dump") command to examine them further.

For example, to see the boot sector of a 720-KB disk, enter the command *d 100*. To see the first FAT of a 1.2-MB disk, enter *d 300*; to see the second copy of the FAT, enter *d f00*. To see the root directory of a 1.4-MB disk, enter *d 2700*.

According to the size of your disk, enter the Dump command that displays the first FAT, and then the second FAT. Note how both FATs contain the

TABLE 8-1. DEBUG ADDRESSES FOR SECRET DISK SNOOPING

Disk Size	ID Byte	Boot Sector	Debug Address	FAT 1	Debug Address	FAT 2	Debug Address	Debug Root Address
360 KB	FD	0	100	1	300	3	700	5	B00
720 KB	F9	0	100	1	300	4	900	7	F00
1.2 MB	F9	0	100	1	300	8	1100	15	1F00
1.4 MB	F0	0	100	1	300	10	1500	19	2700
2.8 MB	F0	0	100	1	300	18	2500	37	4B00

same thing: the initial byte indicates the size of the disk—the ID bytes shown in Table 8-1—then five bytes of FF, then zeros.

Type the command to display the root directory in memory. You'll see something similar to Figure 8-1. (If you see more than two filenames, the extra name will be the disk's volume label.)

You'll see your two files in memory, according to the structure and format of the MS-DOS root directory. Included is the name of the file, its attributes, its date and time, and a key entry showing where the file is located in the FAT.

1. Use the Q command to quit Debug and return to MS-DOS.

2. Delete the file TEST2:

   ```
   C> del a:test2
   ```

3. Return to Debug and reload the first several sectors from the disk.

   ```
   debug
   -l 100 0 0 26
   -
   ```

You'll see what MS-DOS doesn't do when it deletes a file.

Use the proper value from Table 8-1 to view the root directory. You'll see something similar to Figure 8-2.

Note that the only difference between Figure 8-1 and Figure 8-2 is in the first character of the TEST2 filename. The character has been changed to the E5 character. According to MS-DOS, the file has been deleted. Yet its directory entry still has a "stub" or "tombstone" showing the file's name, date, and time, plus the link to the FAT. The first thing MS-DOS does

```
1E1B:0B00  54 45 53 54 31 20 20 20-20 20 20 20 00 00 00 00   TEST1      ....
1E1B:0B10  00 00 00 00 00 00 44 98-47 17 02 00 10 00 00 00   ......D.G......
1E1B:0B20  54 45 53 54 32 20 20 20-20 20 20 20 00 00 00 00   TEST2      ....
1E1B:0B30  00 00 00 00 00 00 47 90-47 17 03 00 16 00 00 00   ......G.G......
```

Figure 8-1. *The root directory of a 360-KB disk.*

```
1E1B:0B00  54 45 53 54 31 20 20 20-20 20 20 20 00 00 00 00   TEST1      ....
1E1B:0B10  00 00 00 00 00 00 44 98-47 17 02 00 10 00 00 00   ......D.G......
1E1B:0B20  E5 45 53 54 32 20 20 20-20 20 20 20 00 00 00 00   .EST2      ....
1E1B:0B30  00 00 00 00 00 00 47 98-47 17 03 00 16 00 00 00   ......G.G......
```

Figure 8-2. *The root directory after deleting the TEST2 file.*

when it "deletes" a file is change the first character in the file's name to E5 in the directory.

Next, enter the proper Debug Dump command to display the first FAT in memory. (Refer to Table 8-1 for the size of disk you're using.) The first byte is still the ID byte, and the next three bytes are all FF. The fifth byte, however, is 0F. This is how MS-DOS shows available disk space. When you deleted TEST2, you also cleared its place markers in the FAT.

To summarize, MS-DOS does two things when it deletes a file:

1. It changes the first letter in the directory to character E5.

2. It marks the file's sectors as available in the FAT.

What MS-DOS does *not* do is go to the file's data on disk and "scrub" the bytes clean. The file's data, and most of the information about the file, remains unaltered on the disk.

You'll need a smart utility to bring the file back to life. You could use Debug to do this manually—but do so only with these small example files: First, change the fifth and sixth bytes in both copies of the FAT to FF. Then, in the root directory, change the first letter in the filename back to T (54 hex). Use the E (Edit memory) command to do this—but only if you're familiar with using Debug.

Save your changes with the following command:

```
-w 100 0 0 26
```

If you don't want to save your changes, that's okay. The MS-DOS Undelete command can get the file back if you want. Debug is useful for recovering one short file at the front of a disk, but for major file recovery on a hard drive, forget it!

Use the Q command to quit Debug and return to MS-DOS. If you manually recovered the TEST2 file, be sure it's okay:

```
C>type a:test2
```

If you tried to undelete the file using Debug and were unsuccessful, take heart. This operation is complex, which will only make you appreciate the MS-DOS Undelete command even more. If you couldn't recover the file, reformat the disk.

Undeleting Without Mirror's Deletion Tracking

The Undelete command works best when the Mirror deletion-tracking option is turned on. For information about Mirror deletion tracking, see Chapter 3. Recovery is possible without Mirror, but it's not as elegant.

If you've just deleted a file, use the Undelete command followed by the file's name. For example:

```
C>undelete config.sys
```

Undelete first checks to see if deletion tracking is installed. If so, the file is quickly recovered—if it can be recovered. If the file cannot be recovered, MS-DOS scans for deleted files to match the name you entered:

```
Directory: C:\
File Specifications: CONFIG.SYS

    Deletion-tracking file not found.

    MS-DOS directory contains     1 deleted files.
    Of those,    1 files may be recovered.

Using the MS-DOS directory.
```

In this example, Undelete tells you that deletion tracking was not installed. However, by looking in the directory, similar to what you did with Debug earlier in this chapter, MS-DOS does locate one matching deleted file. And according to MS-DOS, that file can be fully recovered. Next you'll see the file's directory information:

```
?ONFIG   SYS      682 10-04-92  9:13a  ...A  Undelete (Y/N)?
```

Because MS-DOS doesn't know the first letter of the filename, a question mark is displayed. To recover the file, press Y. MS-DOS prompts you to enter the first letter of the filename. Do so, and then you'll see:

```
File successfully undeleted.
```

The file has been recovered. You can use the Undelete command by itself to scan a complete subdirectory for deleted files. Undelete displays the deleted files, one at a time, along with the file's statistics, and then asks if you want to recover the file.

Note that not all files can be recovered. The odds of getting a file back are inversely proportional to the number of changes you've made to the disk since using the Del or Erase commands. Although the file still has pieces on the disk, the FAT shows that space as "unused." MS-DOS might place a new file in that area, overwriting the existing file. If this occurs, you'll see the following:

```
    ** ?ONFIG   SYS       710 10-03-92  5:16p  ...A
Starting cluster is unavailable. This file cannot be
recovered with the UNDELETE command. Press any key to
continue.
```

The file's "tombstone" is still in the directory, but the FAT shows that some other file is using its space on disk. The file cannot be recovered. This illustrates an important rule about the Undelete command: Undelete a file as soon as possible after deleting it.

Undeleting with Mirror's Deletion Tracking

When you've activated the Mirror deletion tracking feature, using the Undelete command is a snap. Remember, however, that the basic rule is still true: Undelete a file as soon as possible after deleting it. Other than that, Undelete takes on a new face, thanks to the Mirror utility.

To undelete a file with deletion tracking, use the Undelete command and specify the file you want to recover. For example:

```
C>undelete config.sys
```

Undelete gets really happy when it discovers deletion tracking is turned on. Deletion tracking keeps track of a file's name and other important information that aids in the recovery process, as shown here:

```
Directory: C:\
File Specifications: CONFIG.SYS

    Deletion-tracking file contains   1 deleted files.
    Of those,    1 files have all clusters available,
                 0 files have some clusters available,
                 0 files have no clusters available.

    MS-DOS directory contains    1 deleted files.
    Of those,    1 files may be recovered.
```

```
Using the deletion-tracking file.
     CONFIG   SYS      682 10-04-92  9:13a  ...A
     Deleted: 10-09-92 10:33a
All of the clusters for this file are available.
     Undelete (Y/N)?
```

Using the deletion-tracking file, the Undelete command immediately recognizes the deleted file, and the possibility of recovery is good; Undelete displays *1 files have all clusters available*, which means the file hasn't been overwritten in the FAT. Further, the first character of the filename is known. To recover the file, all you need to do is press Y.

```
File successfully undeleted.
```

With deletion tracking, undeleting a group of files using a wildcard is also a snap; you simply keep pressing Y for each file the Undelete command displays. If a file's clusters have been used, you'll see the following:

```
  ** CONFIG   SYS      682 10-04-92  9:13a  ...A
     Deleted: 10-08-92 10:33a
None of the clusters for this file are available.
The file cannot be recovered. Press any key to continue.
```

The Undelete Command's Options

The Undelete command has two sets of options: the /LIST and /ALL options, and the /DT and /DOS options. You can specify one from each set.

The /LIST switch tells Undelete to do a dry run. Using /LIST, you can see which files can be undeleted in a given directory. For example:

```
C>undelete /list | more
```

Use the More filter in case the list of files available for recovery scrolls off the screen. If any filename has an asterisk (*) or double asterisk (**) by it, chances for recovery are slim to nonexistent.

The /ALL switch tells the Undelete command to recover all files that can be recovered. If deletion tracking is turned on, the files will be rescued automatically. If deletion tracking is turned off, Undelete will recover files, but it will use the # character as the first letter in each filename. You must go back later to rename the files.

In the following example, the /ALL switch is used with Undelete to recover the CONFIG.SYS file.

```
C>undelete config.sys /all
```

To recover from an accidental *del *.** command, you can use the following commands:

```
C>undelete *.* /all
```

Note that you cannot specify both /LIST and /ALL in a single Undelete command.

The /DOS and /DT switches are override options. If you specify /DOS, Undelete will ignore the deletion-tracking file. If you specify /DT, Undelete will be forced to use the deletion-tracking file. When would you want to ignore the deletion-tracking file? If the deletion-tracking file is old or corrupt, use the *undelete /dos* command.

Note that you cannot specify both /MS-DOS and /DT with a single Undelete command. You can, however, specify either /ALL or /LIST with either /DOS or /DT.

UNFORMATTING DISKS

Being able to unformat a disk is a miracle. Accidentally formatting a floppy disk is common, and can be a disaster. Always label your disks, so you'll know before you stick the disk in the drive whether or not it contains important files.

When hard-disk drives first became available, they were often accidentally erased. Users weren't stupid, but they were careless. The main reason for all the accidents, however, was that the Format command didn't require a drive letter; it formatted the current drive. So, although you meant to format the floppy disk in drive A, MS-DOS would format drive C (the hard disk) when you typed in *format* and pressed Enter. Later updates to the Format command added warning messages when you attempted to reformat the hard disk, as shown on the next page.

```
WARNING, ALL DATA ON NON-REMOVABLE DISK
DRIVE C: WILL BE LOST!
Proceed with Format (Y/N)?
```

Some versions of MS-DOS offer further protection by requiring you to enter the disk's volume label before proceeding. Yet even with all these safety features, users sometimes reformat their hard disks. And they accidentally reformat floppy disks at about the same rate. Fortunately, the Unformat command makes recovery possible, if not 100 percent guaranteed.

How Can a Disk Be Unformatted?

The MS-DOS Format command has two modes of operation. In the first mode, Format creates tracks and sectors on a new disk. It then creates the boot sector, builds the two FATs, and makes an empty root directory. The formerly blank disk is then ready for MS-DOS to use.

In the second mode, Format "quasi-reformats" an already-formatted disk. Seeing that the disk is already formatted, Format rebuilds the boot sector, erases both FATs, and creates an empty root directory. The disk is then verified—not erased. If any bad sectors are found, they are marked in the FAT. The bulk of the disk—and any data on it—remains untouched, making it possible for the Unformat command to recover the disk.

Note: The Format command's /Q switch takes this concept one step further. When you use the Format command with /Q, Format erases only the boot sector, FAT, and root directory; it doesn't scan for bad sectors. That's why formatting happens so quickly. Because there is no verification, you should use the /Q switch only on newer disks or those without questionable sectors.

Using some tricky maneuvers, the Unformat command can scan a freshly formatted disk, looking for keys that will tell it how to unformat the disk. Eventually, it can locate files and subdirectories that were previously located in the root directory. After rebuilding these files and subdirectories, and then resurrecting the FAT, the rest of the disk is fully recovered. This operation takes some time, but because MS-DOS hasn't really erased the disk, it's possible.

Like undeleting a file, unformatting a disk is a time-critical operation. The sooner you unformat after reformatting, the more successful you'll be. You could wait years before unformatting. But remember, any changes you make to the reformatted disk ruin your chances of recovering the disk.

There is one other instance where Unformat cannot recover a disk: When you use the Format command with the /U (unconditional) switch, the Format command performs an initial, destructive format of the disk. Recovery is not possible.

Unformatting a Disk

Beginning with MS-DOS 5, when you reformat a disk, special unformatting information is saved. You'll see the following when you use the Format command:

```
Checking existing disk format.
Saving UNFORMAT information.
```

MS-DOS first checks to see if the disk is formatted. If it is, MS-DOS saves special unformatting information which can quickly be located by the Unformat command, leading to a faster recovery.

MS-DOS proceeds to format the disk, which is basically a verification process. You'll see the percentage indicator move from 0 to 100 percent as the disk is checked for bad sectors.

To use the Unformat command, type *unformat* followed by the drive letter. For example:

```
C>unformat a:
```

MS-DOS instructs you to insert a disk into drive A. Insert a disk and then press Enter. You'll see a warning message, as shown in Figure 8-3 on the next page.

The message warns that you should use the Unformat command only to recover a formatted disk. It's not a disk vitalizing or undeleting command. Using Unformat is serious business.

If you press Y, Unformat searches the disk for the MIRROR.FIL file, created when you used the Mirror command on the disk. (For more information

```
Restores the system area of your disk by using the image file created
by the MIRROR command.

    WARNING !!        WARNING !!

This command should be used only to recover from the inadvertent use of
the FORMAT command or the RECOVER command. Any other use of the UNFORMAT
command may cause you to lose data! Files modified since the MIRROR image
file was created may be lost.

Searching disk for MIRROR image.

The last time the MIRROR or FORMAT command was used was at 16:54 on 10-08-92.

The MIRROR image file has been validated.

Are you sure you want to update the system area of your drive A (Y/N)?
```

Figure 8-3. *The Unformat command's initial warning message.*

about Mirror, refer to Chapter 3.) If MIRROR.FIL is not found, the date the disk was formatted will be given. You will be asked if you want to recover the disk. Press Y. A few spins of the drive, and the disk is fully recovered.

If the disk was protected with Mirror, you might see two dates displayed: the last time Mirror or Format was used and the *prior* time Mirror or Format was used. Always pick the latest date.

```
If you wish to use the last file as indicated
above, press L. If you wish to use the prior
file as indicated above, press P. Press ESC
to cancel UNFORMAT.
```

Press L or P, according to the date and time of the file. Why choose one or the other? Because an older MIRROR file could be inaccurate. Recovery using an inaccurate MIRROR file would be disastrous. If you know that both files are bad, press the Esc key.

When you press L or P, the disk will be fully recovered in a snap. When prompted, press Y to recover the disk. If you backed out and have decided not to use the MIRROR file, reissue the Unformat command, but this time add the /U switch. The /U switch tells Unformat to ignore the MIRROR files and use a slower MS-DOS recovery method instead.

After the recovery process is complete, you'll see the message, *You may need to restart the system*. Unless you've recovered your hard disk, ignore this message. If you recovered your hard disk, reset.

RESTORING FILES AND SUBDIRECTORIES

Between undeleting files and unformatting disks exists a wide, barren area. Nothing fills the gap; there is no MS-DOS command that quickly restores subdirectories or great branches of a hard disk's tree structure. This might be because there is no simple command to delete subdirectories: You must manually change to each directory with Cd, enter *del *.**, change to the parent directory, and then use Rd to remove the directory you just cleared out. Yet, accidental tree pruning can occur, so it's nice to be able to get some files back.

Basically, there is no command that recovers a subdirectory. If you remove a subdirectory with the Rmdir or Rd command, the Undelete command will not be able to find that subdirectory or recover it. No MS-DOS command can do that. There is, however, the Restore command. If you have a fresh backup disk set handy, Restore will quickly rebuild lost subdirectories. Presently, using Restore is the only way you can recover part of your directory tree using MS-DOS.

Restoring Individual Files

Undeleting files in a subdirectory is possible using the Undelete command. For example:

```
C>undelete *.* /all
```

This command recovers all files in a subdirectory. But you shouldn't rely upon this command too much. If you have a recent backup handy, you can restore files in a specific directory using Restore. For example:

```
C>restore a: c:\word\work\*.* /s
```

In this example, Restore rebuilds all files in the C:\WORD\WORK directory—plus all subdirectories under that directory, thanks to the /S switch. You must insert the backup disks one by one into drive A, beginning with the first backup disk.

Any individual file can be rescued from a backup disk. Simply specify its name using the Restore command in the following format:

restore a: *filename*

The *filename* must specify a full pathname, including the drive letter, colon, and any subdirectories. Wildcards are okay. If you want to verify that the file is current, you can specify a recent date using this format:

restore a: *filename* /a:*date*

Again, *filename* should be a full pathname. The /A switch is followed by a colon and the desired date. The Restore command will restore only *filename*, or files matching that wildcard, backed up on or after the specified date. For example:

```
C>restore c:\word\work\chapter8.doc /a:10-18-92
```

In this example, Restore copies the file CHAPTER8.DOC only if it was backed up on 10-18-92 or later. Note that the date is the date of the file, not the date of the backup or the date of any matching file that might already be on disk.

Generally speaking, Undelete will recover almost any freshly deleted file. If a file cannot be recovered, however, using the Restore command is the next best thing.

Restoring Subdirectories and Branches

If you tear through the subdirectory structure and accidentally remove one or more subdirectories, the only way to get them back is with the Restore command. If the backup is recent, then recovery will be almost full.

To restore a subdirectory branch, use the following command:

restore a: *path**.* /s

In this example, the Restore command copies from drive A all files and directories under the main directory indicated by *path**.*. For example, if you want to restore all the deleted subdirectories and files under the FINANCES directory, use this command:

```
C>restore a: c:\finances\*.* /s
```

Suppose, as is often the case, that a recent backup isn't available. Today is Thursday and the last full disk backup was done last Friday. However, incremental backups were done each day. This means that a full recovery is possible, one step at a time.

The first step is to issue the full Restore command for the missing sub-directory or branch. For example, using the full hard-disk backup disk from last Friday, you enter:

```
C>restore a: c:\finances\*.* /s
```

This restores the hard disk to the state it was in last Friday. To rebuild the disk back to Wednesday night's condition, you must restore incrementally for each day of the week. First, use Monday's incremental backup disk set and enter the following:

```
C>restore a: c:\finances\*.* /s /m
```

The /M switch restores only those files modified since the last backup. Use the same command with Tuesday's and Wednesday's backup disk sets. Then your hard disk will be in the condition it was in the day before the branch was accidentally deleted. No further recovery is possible; you must manually correct the files. I know, it's a pain. But it's much better than having to reconstruct a few weeks' worth of files.

Restoring One or More Hard Disks

You can also use the Restore command to fully restore a hard disk. This instance is quite rare, however, and it will happen only in cases when you've repartitioned a hard disk and are restoring files to it, or when you've upgraded to a new hard-disk drive, replacing an old model. If you've accidentally reformatted a hard disk, you can also try the Restore command, but it's much easier to use Unformat instead.

To restore a full hard disk, use the following command:

```
C>restore a: c:\*.* /s
```

Drive A will hold the backup disks; drive C is the drive to which you're restoring files; *.* tells the Restore command to restore all the files; and the /S switch restores all files in all subdirectories under the root.

Because the MS-DOS Backup and Restore programs work only with one drive at a time, you must use additional commands to restore other hard-disk drives. For example:

```
C>restore a: d:\*.* /s
```

If you're reconstructing a hard disk that has had several incremental back-ups since the last full backup, use the full Restore command first with the full backup set. Then continue with each individual incremental backup set, using the following Restore command:

```
C>restore a: c:\*.* /s /m
```

The /M switch directs the Restore command to add only those files modi-fied since the last backup. Use this command for each incremental backup disk set created since the previous full hard-disk backup. (If you need to incrementally restore any additional hard disks, use the same command but with the proper drive letter.)

If you've done any work-area backups, they should be restored as well. Use the Restore command that restores only the directories or files that you backed up. For example:

```
C>restore a: c:\work\project\*.*
```

In this example, the Restore command copies only those files originally in the C:\WORK\PROJECT directory. If you've used the Xcopy command to archive your work files, you can use Xcopy to copy them back:

```
C>xcopy a: c:\work\project\*.* /s
```

With either Xcopy or Restore, the command to place the files back on the hard disk is the opposite of the command used to back up the files; only the drive letters and pathname are switched.

THE MOTHER OF ALL CRASHES: THE HARD-DISK DRIVE

Almost anything in a computer can bring it to its knees. Minor hiccups can force you to reset. No one knows what causes them. Yet, after reset-ting, you check out your system and everything is okay. It's when the sys-tem *doesn't* come back after resetting that you have to worry.

Your main concern is the hard-disk drive and all its data. Even having done a full hard-disk backup only an hour earlier isn't comforting enough.

This is why I call a hard-disk–drive crash *The Big One*. And it's why getting the disk drive back is always your top priority.

The first step is to examine the causes. Refer to Chapter 7 to see if any other hardware may be responsible for the crash. A blown power supply can stop a PC. Thankfully, it won't bring down the entire system; you can replace the power supply and keep going. If you're certain the problem is the hard-disk drive, read through the following sections.

What Not to Do

When your hard-disk drive crashes, allow yourself some time to panic, but don't do anything rash. No matter what your first instinct is, follow these guidelines:

■ Don't use the Recover command.

   The Recover command does more harm than good.

■ Don't create any new files.

   You might get the hard-disk drive back up again but find that all the files are missing! If so, don't create any new files! New files might overwrite old files that still exist on the disk, but are hidden. And don't install any recovery software on the hard disk; run the recovery program from floppy disks.

■ If you suspect a virus, don't back up.

   A virus might have caused your system to crash and data to be lost. If so, this is not the time to back up. (For more information about viruses, refer to Chapter 9.)

■ Don't immediately do anything.

   Don't rush and try the Unformat command on the disk. In fact, don't use Unformat on any crashed disk. Unformat is designed only for recovering from a recent disk format operation.

Dealing with the Unthinkable

The best way to deal with a hard-disk–drive crash is to follow the MS-DOS boot process from hitting the power switch all the way through AUTOEXEC.BAT. The object is to find the element that's gone haywire.

Your PC's hardware will often inform you when the hard-disk drive is AWOL. Why doesn't MS-DOS? Because MS-DOS hasn't been loaded. Therefore, based on your hardware, the types of error messages you might see will vary:

```
Unable to load operating system
```

```
Hard drive not available
```

```
Error: Check Setup program, press <F1> to continue
```

```
IBM ROM Basic
```

The last message (*IBM ROM Basic*) appeared with the earliest PCs. If there wasn't a disk handy, the PC dropped into a ROM BASIC interpreter. In any case, the hard-disk drive wasn't found by the BIOS bootstrapping routine, so the computer sat and waited.

Sometimes your computer may prompt you to insert a boot disk. If so, use the Emergency Boot Disk: Place it in drive A, press Enter, and then start troubleshooting.

If you simply see the error message and nothing else happens, put the Emergency Boot Disk into drive A and reset.

Take Stock of the Situation

Your first thoughts should be about what just happened. How did the crash come about?

Timing is everything in a PC. If the hard-disk drive doesn't come up when you first boot your computer in the morning, the problem could simply be a downed hard-disk drive. Or the drive could be cold. Some older drives need to warm up a bit, so waiting a few minutes might temporarily solve the problem. (However, a slow-in-the-morning hard-disk drive should be replaced.)

If the hard-disk drive doesn't come up after a power outage, some electrical "nasty" might have killed it. It could be the controller or a chip on the hard-disk drive. In any event, you'll need to have your computer checked. Don't give up; keep checking the items mentioned here to see if you can get something from the drive.

Did you make any modifications to CONFIG.SYS? Some hard drives require special device drivers. In an overzealous editing session, you might have removed these commands. To remedy the situation, you should boot with the Emergency Boot Disk, use Edlin or your text editor to repair the CONFIG.SYS file, and then reset.

Finally, determine which programs you were running before the crash. Some older MS-DOS utilities might not be 100-percent compatible with your version of MS-DOS. Disk caches might interfere with the hard-disk drive or write sectors improperly. Your boot sector or partition table might have been accidentally erased.

Check the CMOS

After diagnosing the problem, run your computer's Setup program to access the battery–backed-up memory, or CMOS. On some systems, this involves running a program. On others, you access the Setup program using a special key combination.

The computer might prompt you to check the CMOS memory. In some cases, when a hard-disk–drive error is detected, your PC will display an error message and ask you to press F1 (or Esc) to edit the system configuration. If so, press the proper keys and check your system's setup.

While reading Chapter 1, you should have recorded your system's setup in Appendix A. Compare those values with what you see on your screen. Figure 8-4 on the next page shows a sample Setup program.

Check the hard-disk–drive entries. Is anything there? If not, use the key commands in your Setup program to assign the proper type to your hard drive. For example, if your hard-disk drive was type 17 but now the Setup program says *not installed*, change the setting back to type 17.

Save your changes to the CMOS memory, and then reset your computer. If the hard-disk drive comes back—great! If not, continue with the Emergency Boot Disk in drive A.

If you notice that a CMOS or Setup problem occurs on a consistent basis—for example, you lose the hard-disk drive each time you turn off the PC—you might need a new system battery. Another telltale sign is

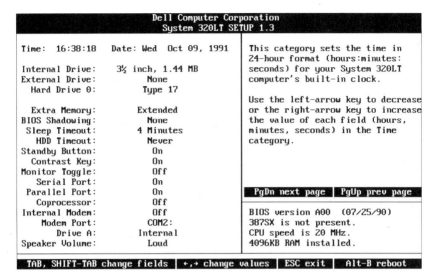

Figure 8-4. *A 386 laptop PC's Setup program.*

that your system loses track of the time. Simply order another battery from your dealer.

Use the Emergency Boot Disk

With the Emergency Boot Disk in drive A, you can try to access the hard-disk drive:

```
EBD>c:
```

If you see the error message *Invalid drive specification*, drive C isn't with us. Move on to the next section, "Check the Partition Table."

If you don't see an error message, you've accessed drive C. Prove it by using the Cd command:

```
EBD>cd
C:\
```

Enter *dir* to check for files on the disk. If you can see the files and everything looks okay, remove the Emergency Boot Disk and then reset your system. Your hard drive is okay.

If the files appear scrambled or random characters appear after you type the Dir command, you might have a boot-sector problem. You might need to run the Unformat command to restore the boot sector. Change back to drive A and use the Emergency Boot Disk.

Check the Partition Table

From the Emergency Boot Disk in drive A, run the Fdisk program. Select item number 4, Display Partition Information. The next screen should list the partitions for your hard-disk drive. At least one PRI DOS, or primary MS-DOS, partition should be shown. Other partitions might be non-DOS or EXT (extended) partitions.

If all your hard-disk drives appear, and the size in megabytes is equal to the size of your hard-disk drives, move to the next section, "Check the System Area."

If Fdisk tells you that you have an *Invalid partition table* or any other error, you can rebuild the partition table using the Unformat command (providing that you've saved your partition table using the mirror /partn command). The file PARTNSAV.FIL should already be on your Emergency Boot Disk. If so, enter the following at the prompt:

`EBD>unformat /partn`

Unformat will prompt you to insert the disk containing PARTNSAV.FIL. This disk should already be in the drive, so press Enter.

Next, Unformat displays the date of the PARTNSAV.FIL file, then a map of the current partition table. To restore the table, press 1, the letter of the drive you want to restore, or A to restore all hard drives.

After Unformat restores the partition table, reset your system (if it doesn't reset automatically). If your PC comes up in its normal fashion, pay homage to the authors of MS-DOS. If there are still problems, keep reading.

Check the System Area

The system area of a hard disk is the boot sector, the FAT, and the root directory. Every logical drive in your system will have its own system area, as opposed to one main partition table. If your hard disk's partition table is intact, you should be able to access your hard-disk drives.

If you encounter errors when accessing a drive, it still might be a partition-table problem. Use Fdisk to examine your partition table again and to verify that the partition or logical drive is installed on your system. If not, use the *undelete /partn* command as described in the previous section to restore your hard disk's partitions.

If you can access all of drive C, but the computer won't boot from drive C, all you might need to do is transfer the system to drive C. Do this with the Sys command:

```
EBD>sys c:
```

After a few moments, you'll see the message *System transferred*. Reset and boot from your hard disk to continue.

If you have problems accessing your hard disk (for example, garbled files in the root directory), you might need to reinstall the system area with the Unformat command.

If you have Mirror installed, and the version of the MIRROR.FIL file is recent, recovery will be smooth. For instructions, refer to the section "Unformatting a Disk," earlier in this chapter.

If the hard-disk drive has never had Mirror installed, or if the drive was formatted under a previous version of MS-DOS, you can still use the Unformat command. The secret is to use the /U switch. This makes recovery painfully slow, and the files in the root directory will be given generic names, but it works:

```
EBD>unformat c: /u
```

Use this command only if drive C has garbled files or if the disk appears to be empty when you know it contains files. Expect the operation to take anywhere from 10 minutes to over an hour.

Rebuilding from the Ground Up

If you've tried everything—the Setup program and the CMOS, rebuilding the partition tables, using Unformat—and nothing worked, you'll need to rebuild the hard disk from the ground up. (This assumes, of course, that it isn't hardware failure causing the problem. If it is a hardware problem, have a disk doctor troubleshoot your hard-disk drive and controller. If the drive cannot be fixed, or if you opt to replace the drive, you are back to the point of rebuilding from scratch.)

The following steps will effectively restore any hard-disk drive to working order. Or, if you're starting out with a new hard-disk drive, follow these instructions for setting up the drive. Note that this will be completely successful only if you have a recent backup disk handy. If not, you'll have to manually reinstall all your software.

Follow these five steps to rebuild your hard disk (or to set up a new hard-disk drive) from the ground up:

1. Perform a low-level format.

2. Partition with Fdisk.

3. Perform a high-level format.

4. Install MS-DOS.

5. Restore data.

Performing a Low-Level Format

You have two ways to initially format a disk: You can use the special formatting utility that came with the drive, or you can use Debug to access the drive's ROM and then reformat manually. Both of these methods work on the majority of PC hard-disk drives: MFM, RLL, and ESDI drives can be formatted either using Debug or with special software; SCSI drives must be handled with special software.

If you have an IDE drive, which is the case with most laptops, you can skip the low-level formatting step. All IDE drives come with low-level formatting from the factory. There is no way to do it yourself. In fact, if an IDE drive somehow loses its format, you should return the drive to your dealer for formatting or buy a new drive.

If your hard-disk drive has a low-level formatting program, run it to initialize the disk with a low-level format. This format is "destructive"; it initializes the entire disk. The program will warn you that you cannot recover from this type of formatting. But everything is okay because you are starting from scratch.

If your hard-disk drive lacks its own initialization program, you can use Debug. Actually, you use Debug to access the formatting program on the hard-disk controller's ROM. Start Debug:

```
EBD>debug
```

There are three Debug commands to access your hard drive's controller. The most common is the following:

```
g=c800:5
```

That's G, for "Go," then an equal sign and the address C800:5. After pressing Enter, you'll find yourself in the hard-disk controller's low-level formatting program. Follow the instructions you see on the screen and proceed with any default options as displayed. Your system might reset after the low-level format is complete.

If this command doesn't work, you might have to reset. After resetting, you can restart Debug after your system starts up again, and then try either of the following commands:

```
g=c800:6
```

Or:

```
g=c800:ccc
```

Either of these commands might work, depending on the hard-drive controller. If both commands fail, you'll need to contact your dealer or the hard-drive manufacturer for assistance.

Partitioning with Fdisk

After the disk is low-level formatted, you should partition it using the Fdisk command. Run Fdisk:

```
EBD>fdisk
```

From Fdisk's main menu, select option 1, Create DOS Partition or Logical DOS Drive.

Note: *If you're working with a second hard-disk drive, first select option 5, Change Current Fixed Disk Drive.*

Follow the steps you see on the screen, partitioning the drive into logical drives if necessary. If the hard-disk drive is your boot disk, drive C, make it a PRI DOS, or primary MS-DOS, drive. Other hard-disk drives can be EXT DOS, or extended MS-DOS partitions, which will not be bootable.

Generally, pressing Enter while in Fdisk will always take you down the proper path. Eventually, you'll press Esc to exit. Your system will reset and load the new partition table into memory. Remember to keep your Emergency Boot Disk in drive A until you've made the hard disk a boot disk (as shown in the next section).

Performing a High-Level Format

After partitioning, the disk is ready for high-level formatting using the Format command. The Format command places the boot sector, FAT, and root directory on the disk. Then, as with an already-formatted floppy disk, Format verifies your hard disk's low-level format.

If you're formatting drive C, you'll want to make it a boot disk. Use the following Format command:

```
EBD>format c: /s
```

The /S switch directs Format to put the MS-DOS system files, IO.SYS and MSDOS.SYS, as well as COMMAND.COM, on the hard disk. To format any hard-disk drive other than drive C, remove the /S switch.

Use the Format command on every hard disk you've partitioned. For example, if you have drive D, E, or higher, use Format on each drive:

```
EBD>format d:
```

If you've formatted drive C as your boot disk, take a second to test it. Remove the Emergency Boot Disk from drive A and reset your PC. Be sure that the hard-disk drive boots properly and loads MS-DOS. If you see the date and time prompts and then "C>," everything's okay. If the hard-disk drive doesn't boot, the system files might not be on it. You can copy the system files from the Emergency Boot Disk to the hard disk using the following command:

```
EBD>sys c:
```

Installing MS-DOS

Installing MS-DOS is necessary only if you're not recovering from a full hard-disk–drive crash. Otherwise, you can simply restore your MS-DOS files at the same time that you restore all your other files. If you've had a full hard-disk–drive crash, skip to the next section, "Restoring Data." But if you're setting up a new hard-disk drive, transfer MS-DOS to your new boot disk, drive C. Obtain the MS-DOS Upgrade kit and place Disk 1 in drive A. Enter *setup* to begin the installation/upgrade process.

Restoring Data

To restore your hard-disk drive's data from all your backup disks, use the following Restore command:

```
EBD>restore a: c:\*.* /s /p
```

The Restore command copies backup files from the disks in drive A to the hard disk, restoring all files in all subdirectories. The /P switch protects your system files (IO.SYS, MSDOS.SYS, and COMMAND.COM); Restore will ask your permission before it overwrites these files.

If you're using a third-party backup program, use it to restore your hard-disk drive.

After restoration is complete, reset one last time. Check out your system to be sure everything is okay. Finally, reconstruct any data that might have been lost due to the crash.

SUMMARY

"The Big One" can be anything from a lost file to a totally dead hard-disk drive. MS-DOS provides solutions for each of these situations: The Undelete command can resurrect dead files; the Unformat command can bring a reformatted disk back to life; and the Restore command can recover just about anything—if you have a recent backup disk handy.

Chapter 9
The Virus

"Virus" is a trendy, ear-catching media word that has taken on a new meaning in the personal computer era. It's like a mental atomic bomb terrorists can bring in from the ether, wreaking more havoc than a roomful of congressmen. And it's personal: a virus can attack your computer and your data—without discretion. Anyone can get The Virus. "Who is safe?" the commentator quizzes. "Who is safe?"

There's no need to panic. True, viruses are deadly and they're real. Yet there are practical ways to prevent them from infecting your system and ways to deal with them if you suspect you are infected. This is nothing to get upset about, no reason to overreact. Nasty computer programs exist, but happily, coping with them is relatively painless.

This chapter is about The Virus. I'm not going to glorify The Virus, explain how viruses work, or discuss the mental limitations of those who create them. Instead, the subject is keeping your PC safe from viruses and other nasty PC programs. And if you suspect that you've caught one, this chapter will tell you how best to deal with it.

WHAT'S A VIRUS AND WHAT'S A SNIFFLE?

Not everything that goes haywire in a computer is due to a virus. With the media jumping up and down and all, it's hard to tell the difference. In fact, some "computer consultants" pull the wool over the eyes of unsuspecting users, tell them they have a virus (when they don't), and charge them money for removal. This is low.

Never assume that what ails you is a virus. It's too easy. Many things can cause a computer to glitch, and some glitches can never be replicated. Viruses, and all their nasty-program cousins, leave telltale markings. They are consistent and fairly obvious to spot. Before diving into the subject any further, the following sections will bring you up to date on virus terminology and technology.

Viral Terminology

How unfortunate that computing has come to a point where we need to concern ourselves with the following terms:

Virus

Virus is the generic name given to a program that causes trouble. Different "strains" of viruses do different nasty things in different degrees. The general term for this type of nasty program is "virus," although specific terms describe different types of malodorous programs. (See the next section.)

Infection

A virus usually invades, or infects, some other, well-meaning program. It attaches itself to that program in some ingenious and hidden manner. When you run the innocent program, the virus will take over, lie low for a while, or try to infect another program. Most viruses that do something nasty will wait a while before performing the deed—which is one way you can stop a virus after you've detected an infection.

Virus Protection

Protecting yourself against a computer virus is like protecting your body against deleterious biological viruses. Here are some simple rules that you can follow:

- Never boot from an unknown floppy disk. Some programs install themselves from their own boot disks, and some games will run only when booted in your floppy-disk drive. That's okay, provided the disk comes sealed, is professionally labeled, and comes from a reputable company.

- Never use software that comes on unlabeled disks. This includes disks containing software you "borrow" from friends. On the other hand, some shareware programs and disks you get from user groups are okay.

■ Do not use pirated software. Taking a look-see at a hot new product is fun, but not if the person who originally pirated the software also installed a virus.

■ Do not allow others to use your computer as a "test system." There's always one guy (or gal) in every office who will want to use your system this way. Although he (or she) may be the sweetest guy (or gal) in the world, just say "no."

■ Follow the good-housekeeping rules in this book. Keep your root directory clean. And back up! Back up! Back up! Also, avoid having extra copies of COMMAND.COM lying around. That's really the only file most viruses infect. The more copies of COMMAND.COM you have, the higher your risk. One copy of COMMAND.COM in the root directory is enough.

Virus Scanner

Virus scanners are special utilities designed to seek out and identify viruses on disk. Some, such as the sample batch-file virus scanner listed later in this chapter, merely check your COM, EXE, and SYS files for illegal modifications. Unfortunately, viruses are smart and sometimes modify files to avoid detection. To hunt down those viruses, you need software that will scan the internals of each file individually, looking for virus *signatures*, or fragments of code, that identify the diabolic programs.

Virus Deletion or Removal

After a virus scanner detects a virus, you should remove the virus. Some software is sophisticated in the way it extracts a virus from an infected program. Most software, however, will totally delete the infected file—filling the sectors the file used with null bytes 10 times over! You can then replace the infected file with an uninfected original, either from the program's distribution disks or from a backup disk.

Other Medical Terms

Virus detection and removal software introduces other "cutsie" terms. Be prepared to be barraged by them. Keep a happy disposition. Such a grave subject often deserves a bit of jocularity.

The Nasty Parade of Programs

The media blitz on the word "virus" has turned it into a rather broad term. There are actually several types of evil programs to contend with.

Trojan Horse

This was the first identified type of "virus." Quite a few early EGA users got stung by a program named EGADEMO.EXE. The program claimed to test the graphics abilities of the new EGA system. While it was amazing the user with pretty colors, it was secretly reformatting the hard disk. When the reformatting was done, the program displayed the message *Arf, Arf! Gotcha!*

EGADEMO.EXE best describes a *Trojan horse*: a program you think does one thing but turns out to do something else, something nefarious. These programs disguise themselves in name only. Sometimes they're clever. For example, one Trojan horse would zap a hard-disk drive only if the disk was more than 50 percent full. Another famous Trojan horse advertised itself as a virus checker!

The best way to deal with a Trojan horse is not to use it. Only run shrink-wrapped software. Shareware or public-domain programs you get from reputable software exchanges and user groups are okay. Beware of everything else.

You can also use utilities that scan for potentially dangerous MS-DOS commands in suspect programs. Some will even lock out key sectors of the hard disk, preventing the sectors from being overwritten. These utilities are designed for general virus protection, but they can easily halt a Trojan horse.

Time Bomb

Like a Trojan horse, a *time bomb* (or *logic bomb*) starts out as a well-meaning program. Some bomb programs even do something constructive. Internally, the time bomb keeps track of the date and time, the number of times you've run the program, or some other event. When you reach a certain date, or have run the program *x* number of times, the time bomb explodes, erasing data and wreaking havoc.

Time bombs started out as a method of enforcing payment to government programming contractors. The bomb would go off after about six weeks, usually displaying some type of error message. (No data would be destroyed.) The programmer would be called, demand payment, fix the time bomb, and everyone would be happy.

Tales in the media tell about disgruntled employees who write time bombs, designing them to explode long after the employee has been terminated. On a PC, this is nothing to worry about unless other people regularly use it. Catching a time bomb in a well-meaning program is tough. In fact, the only real defense is to back up regularly.

Wabbit

The term *wabbit* comes from the Elmer Fudd term that means *rabbit*— furry little creatures that multiply like, well, rabbits. Basically, a wabbit duplicates itself every time it's run, eventually filling up a hard disk. This program doesn't infect other programs and is quite easy to stop: Simply delete all the wabbit files. Wabbits are ware, er, rare on PCs.

Worm

A *worm* is similar to a virus. The difference is that worms tend to live in larger computers and proliferate through computer networks. This makes them especially nasty, because so many big computers (mainframes and minis) are tethered together. In the PC world, worms are rare.

The most famous worm of all was the "Internet" worm, launched by a college computer science student. The worm infected various computers at military, educational, and industrial sites, passing itself through the mail system (known as the Internet). The worm replicated itself and brought the entire nationwide network to a halt.

Virus

A virus is a program that does nasty things, but you never see it by itself. A virus infects another program, actually becoming part of the first program's internal code. Some viruses attempt to proliferate, spreading themselves to other PCs via COMMAND.COM or other system files. But for the most part, a virus simply attaches to a well-meaning program and lays low until it's ready to rip your system to shreds.

WATCHING FOR VIRUSES

How can you tell if your computer's been infected by a virus? The key is to keep an eye on your program files, especially your system files (IO.SYS and MSDOS.SYS) and COMMAND.COM. Most viral infections wait a while before going into action. If you notice any changes in any key files, there's a chance of infection.

You can tell if a file has changed by comparing its current directory listing with a previous listing. If the date and time or file size has changed, and there is no other reasonable explanation for the change, you might have an infection. Most commercial virus-scanning programs will perform this type of test, comparing files on disk with a master record. You can do something similar, though not as sophisticated, using batch files.

Creating a Master File List

MS-DOS has only three types of runnable files (COM, EXE, and SYS files) that can be infected by a virus. Batch files (BAT) can't be infected, but they will often call a COM or EXE file in which a virus might be hidden. None of the other files on your system are suspect; MS-DOS never loads them into memory and executes any code in them. It's possible, but only if a COM, EXE, or SYS file has first been modified to do so.

You can create a master list of all these files on your hard disk by using the Dir command:

```
C>dir \*.com /a /s
```

Using the *.COM (or *.EXE or *.SYS) wildcard combined with the /S switch, the Dir command displays a list of all those files in all directories on the disk. The /A (attribute) switch ensures that all hidden or system files also get listed.

Output from these Dir commands needs to be redirected and appended to a file that then becomes your master program list. Checking for a virus is done by comparing that list with a new list you generate. Any differences, aside from programs deleted or programs added, indicate a change in a file. That's your clue to a possible viral infection.

You can create a batch file called BIGLIST that will build the master program list. The commands for the batch file are listed in Figure 9-1. Create
this batch file using your favorite text editor or the MS-DOS Editor. Save
it as BIGLIST.BAT.

BIGLIST.BAT uses output redirection and the Find command to create a
list of all COM, EXE, and SYS files on a given hard-disk drive. Specify
the drive's letter following the Biglist command at the MS-DOS prompt. If
no drive is specified, Biglist will generate a list for the current drive.

The following line-by-line description explains how BIGLIST.BAT works.
Putting this program to work is discussed in the next section.

Line 1 turns the echo off. Line 2 displays *Creating master list...*, primarily
because the next three lines may take some time to work.

Lines 3, 4, and 5 scan the drive specified by the optional parameter %1 for
COM, EXE, and SYS files. The output is redirected and appended to a file
named $$$ALL.

Line 6 displays the first trimming message.

Line 7 uses the Find command to narrow the list so that it contains only
filenames. One character common to every file listing in a directory is the
colon that appears in the file's time stamp. The Find command in line 7
pares down $$$ALL, redirecting into the file $$$AL1 only those lines con-
taining colons.

Line 8 displays the second trimming message.

```
 1: @echo off
 2: echo Creating master list...
 3: dir %1\*.com /a /s > $$$ALL
 4: dir %1\*.exe /a /s >> $$$ALL
 5: dir %1\*.sys /a /s >> $$$ALL
 6: echo Trimming list, step one...
 7: find ":" $$$ALL > $$$AL1
 8: echo Trimming list, step two...
 9: find /v "Total files" $$$AL1 > $$$AL2
10: echo Trimming list, step three...
11: find /v "Directory of" $$$AL2 > BIGLIST
12: del $$$*
13: echo BIGLIST created.
```

Figure 9-1. *The script for BIGLIST.BAT*

Line 9 trims the list even further by using the Find command's /V switch to remove all lines saying "Total files" in the file $$$AL1 and redirecting output to the file $$$AL2.

Line 10 displays the final trimming message.

Line 11 again uses the Find command's /V switch to remove all the "Directory of" lines from the file and redirects the output to the file BIGLIST. This file will now consist only of filenames, except for three stubs created by the Find command. (Each stub is 10 hyphens followed by the name of the file the Find command scanned.)

Line 12 deletes all the temporary files.

Line 13 displays the final message; the BIGLIST file has been created.

Using BIGLIST.BAT

Run BIGLIST.BAT on your PC. If you have more than one hard-disk drive, run BIGLIST.BAT on each drive to create separate BIGLIST files. Each BIGLIST file will contain a list of all the COM, EXE, and SYS files on that drive.

You can use the Type command to view the contents of the BIGLIST file:

```
C>type biglist | more
```

This BIGLIST file will become your master file list. You'll compare it to later runs of the BIGLIST.BAT file, checking to ensure that they match. Any differences would be the clue that a virus might be present.

To transform the BIGLIST data file into the master list, change its name to MASTER:

```
C>ren biglist master
```

Remember to create separate BIGLIST data files for each of your hard-disk drives. Or, if you want to get fancy, you could "hard code" the batch file to create a *huge* BIGLIST file for all your hard-disk drives. You'd need to add the proper commands to BIGLIST.BAT. However, this would make the batch file very specific to one computer.

```
1: @echo off
2: call biglist.bat %1
3: echo Now checking for different files:
4: pause
5: fc biglist master > vcheck.dat
6: cls
7: type vcheck.dat | more
```

Figure 9-2. *This is the script for VCHECK.BAT*

Now to check for viruses, run the VCHECK.BAT program shown in Figure 9-2. Create this program using your text editor or the MS-DOS Editor. Save it as VCHECK.BAT.

A description of VCHECK.BAT follows.

Line 1 turns the echo off.

Line 2 calls the BIGLIST.BAT program, which creates another BIGLIST data file. Remember to change the name of the original BIGLIST file to MASTER before you run VCHECK.BAT. If you don't, BIGLIST.BAT will overwrite the original BIGLIST file.

When BIGLIST.BAT is finished, Line 3 displays the message *Now checking for different files.*

The Pause command in Line 4 waits for the user to press any key.

Line 5 runs the Fc (file compare) command. It compares the data files BIGLIST and MASTER, redirecting the output to the file VCHECK.DAT.

Line 6 clears the screen, and line 7 displays the VCHECK.DAT file, piping the output through the More filter.

Checking for Viruses with VCHECK.BAT

Running VCHECK.BAT immediately after creating your initial MASTER list doesn't realistically test for viruses. But it will demonstrate how VCHECK runs if it doesn't detect any changes in your files:

```
C>vcheck
Creating master list...
Trimming list, step one...
Trimming list, step two...
Trimming list, step three...
BIGLIST created.
Now checking for different files:
Press any key to continue...
```

When you press a key, the screen clears. Because the BIGLIST file just
created matches your MASTER file list, you'll see the following:

```
Comparing files BIGLIST and MASTER
FC: no differences encountered
```

Suppose you run this command a few weeks down the road, after you did
something bad—you booted from a questionable floppy disk a friend gave
you. After VCHECK clears the screen, you see the following:

```
Comparing files BIGLIST and MASTER
***** BIGLIST
---------- $$$ALL
COMMAND  COM      49670 12-14-93     6:42a
LOTUS    COM       5631 07-19-89     1:23a
***** MASTER
---------- $$$ALL
COMMAND  COM      47845 04-09-91     5:00a
LOTUS    COM       5631 07-19-89     1:23a
*****
```

The Fc command displays any lines that differ between the two files. If
such a line is found, the lines before and after it are also displayed. In this
example, COMMAND.COM is the culprit.

In the BIGLIST file, COMMAND.COM has a size of 49,670 bytes and is
dated 12-14-93 at 6:42 A.M. In the MASTER file, the file you should trust,
COMMAND.COM has a size of 47,845 bytes and is dated 4-9-91 at 5:00
A.M.—which will be the same time shown for all your MS-DOS system
files. Obviously, something rotten has gotten into COMMAND.COM.

Now that you've created them, copy BIGLIST.BAT, the MASTER file, and
VCHECK.BAT to your Emergency Boot Disk. That way you'll be assured
of having a clean MASTER file to check against.

Another Way to Check

In addition to running batch-file scanners, such as VCHECK, or commercial virus scanners, you can also check the date and time of your files.
Most developers give all their program and data files the same date and
time. Some software developers have adapted the hour:minute display in a
directory's entry to tell you the major and minor versions of a program.

For example, in the first release of MS-DOS 5, all files had a time of 5:00 A.M. PC Tools version 7.1 shows all its files with a time of 7:10 A.M. If you scan a directory listing and notice that some files have different times—especially MS-DOS files—something sneaky may be going on.

Of course, there might be a logical explanation for the time difference. Some programs self-modify and update themselves. However, some viruses are smart enough to modify a file's date, time, or size in a manner that makes it look like the file hasn't changed. Sometimes it's impossible to know.

Don't be too quick to jump to the "I-have-the-virus" conclusion. But if you're seriously in doubt, buy a third-party virus scanner that will internally check a file for virus signatures.

The Most Disappointing News

You can check for viruses all day long. But like fighting snails in the garden, it's an uphill battle. I recommend checking for changed files by using VCHECK at least once a month; immediately before you back up is a good time to check. If something starts going crazy, however, or you notice files are missing, notice a drive magically reformatted, or you see strange messages, you probably have an infection.

Viruses affect your computer in a variety of ways. Being able to spot a true virus from a recurring bug is a bit of an art. If you follow the advice offered throughout this book and nothing seems to explain your PC's odd behavior, then it's likely that you have a virus. (Remember to note any changes in CONFIG.SYS; goofs there can cause virus-like behavior.)

If you suspect you have a virus, your job is to locate and remove it. The next few sections show you how.

VIRUS REMOVAL

You have a virus, you know it's a virus, and furthermore, you know which files are infected. If it is truly a virus, you've probably seen some telltale message. The first nationally publicized virus appeared on quite a few

Apple Macintoshes several years back to celebrate the anniversary of the Mac II. It was harmless, but it brought to light the potential for havoc a virus can bring.

What to Do and What Not to Do

When you suspect a virus, the first thing to do is to boot from a pristine boot disk, such as your Emergency Boot Disk.

If the hard disk was totally wiped out by the virus, restore the disk. This might involve a complete restoration, starting with low-level formatting. The best course of action to take is the same one you would for a total hard-disk–drive crash. Refer to "The Mother of All Crashes: The Hard-Disk Drive," in Chapter 8.

Only the nastiest of viruses will erase your hard disk. Some of them may only corrupt the boot sector where the partition tables are kept. That's extremely common; the partition tables are easy to access, quick to erase, and can cause the most damage. If that's your situation, you can restore the partition tables using the *unformat /partn* command from your Emergency Boot Disk. Refer to "Check the Partition Table," in Chapter 8.

If your hard disk is still intact, be careful about what you do. Above all, *don't back up!* Assume that your backup disks—especially your most recent full-disk backup—are virus-free. You don't want to taint them by backing up the virus.

If you want, use the Copy command to copy data files to a separate disk. Be sure that disk is already formatted, or format it using the Format command on your Emergency Boot Disk. This isn't necessary, but if it gives you peace of mind, go ahead. Remember, don't back up. Also, avoid running any software on the hard-disk drive.

Locating a Virus

Relatively tame viruses might only display a nasty message, affect typing, or prevent data files from being saved. If you suspect one of these viruses, run the VCHECK batch file or a commercial virus scanner to help you locate the infected file.

Remember that VCHECK uses the Fc (file compare) command to locate files with different sizes and time or date stamps. The Fc command displays an extra line above and below any differing lines of text it finds. If VCHECK shows you three files, don't suspect all three; only the middle file is different.

I suggest that you should get a printed copy of the list VCHECK creates. Use this command:

```
EBD>copy vcheck.dat > prn
```

Mark on the hardcopy each of the files VCHECK locates. Key files such as IO.SYS, MS-DOS.SYS (or their IBM-named siblings, IBMBIO.COM and IBMDOS.COM), and COMMAND.COM are the most suspect. Any changes in them indicate infection.

Changes in other files should be examined as well. Keep in mind that some COM or EXE files might be self-modifying. However, you might want to proceed with virus-removal steps on these files.

Removing a Virus

To remove a virus, you delete the suspect file. For system files such as IO.SYS and MSDOS.SYS, you must first remove their protected status. Do that with one of the following Attrib commands:

```
C>attrib -r -h -s io.sys
```

Or:

```
C>attrib -r -h -s msdos.sys
```

You can then delete the files from disk. Of course, the Del command doesn't really remove the file. What you should do is totally wipe the file from disk, forcing MS-DOS to replace all its bytes on disk with zeros. Most third-party virus checking programs use such a utility to remove the infected file. Some utility packages, such as Norton and Mace, come with complete file-destroying utilities; use one of them to delete the file.

After the file is deleted, replace it with an uninfected original. To replace system files, use the Sys command from your Emergency Boot Disk:

```
EBD>sys c:
```

The Sys command transfers IO.SYS, MSDOS.SYS, and COMMAND.COM to drive C, replacing the older, infected files.

Note: Do this only if the files on drive C show signs of infection. Reset after using the Sys command to ensure that drive C boots. The virus should be gone.

When the virus is in other, non-system files, you must find an original, untainted copy of the file.

For example, suppose your MOUSE.SYS file, the mouse device driver, is infected. The first step is to delete the infected file:

```
EBD>del c:\mouse\mouse.sys
```

Then replace that file using either a copy from a backup disk or the original copy from the distribution disk. Put your mouse system disk into drive A and enter:

```
EBD>copy mouse.sys c:\mouse\mouse.sys
```

Or, if you have a backup disk handy, use the Restore command:

```
EBD>restore a: c:\mouse\mouse.sys
```

If you're using a third-party backup program, use its own restore command to recover the file.

After copying the original file, verify that it is untainted. Use your hard copy of the VCHECK.DAT file and compare the file's size with the size listed in the MASTER file. The sizes should match. If not, the original or the backup copy might be infected as well. If the backup copy is infected, you should try a previous backup copy or the original distribution disk's copy of the file.

When the distribution copy of a file is tainted, the infection may have occurred when you first installed the program. In that case, you'll need to contact the software developer, tell them what happened, and then order new disks.

After you have replaced your files, test your system. Be sure that the virus has been removed. Run VCHECK or a third-party virus scanner. Test the system for virus-caused quirks. When you are sure that your system is clean, back up.

SUMMARY

Viruses and other nasty things are all a sad part of using a computer. You can avoid them, however, if you follow safe computing practices, the most important of which is avoiding unknown disks and programs.

Above all, keep in mind that not everything that goes awry in a computer is caused by a virus. Computers can be finicky. Floppy-disk drives and hard-disk drives can wander away without any prompting from a virus. If you follow the rules for safe, anti-virus computing, you don't need to suspect a virus. Only after you've checked out your system, referred to this book's troubleshooting guide in Chapter 11, and verified that files have been mysteriously altered, should you consider an infection by a virus or some other nasty program.

The VCHECK batch file in this chapter will help you scan for potential viral infections and remove them. If you really want to be safe, consider using a third-party virus-checking program. And don't panic!

Chapter 10

When To Buy Utilities

Many of the potential problems presented in this book are easily solved using only MS-DOS. But sometimes you might need to augment MS-DOS with other utilities. These special programs supplement MS-DOS and, in many cases, offer surprising solutions for seemingly insolvable problems. Utilities can be time—and data—savers.

This chapter is about third-party utilities—programs you can purchase to boost your PC's performance, safeguard data, and troubleshoot MS-DOS. Several popular utilities are discussed here, in five topic areas:

- Undeleting files
- Defragmenting
- Disk tune-ups
- General repair
- Diagnostics

This chapter isn't meant to be a product guide, nor are comparisons offered. Refer to articles in any of the popular computer magazines if you need that type of information.

THIRD-PARTY UTILITIES FOR MS-DOS

Utilities and operating systems go hand-in-hand. With some operating systems, such as UNIX, it's hard to tell where the operating system ends and the utilities begin. MS-DOS is a little more clear-cut. Generally speaking, external MS-DOS commands, such as Format, Fdisk, Xcopy, and so on, are really utilities. Everything else—basically COMMAND.COM and the two hidden system files—is the actual operating system.

Even with its external commands, MS-DOS doesn't do everything, which is why third-party utilities are often necessary. MS-DOS does more now than it did with version 1.0. Back then, MS-DOS came with just three utility programs: Format, Debug, and Edlin. Today MS-DOS comes with dozens of utilities—including Undelete and Unformat. To plug any MS-DOS functionality holes, you can buy other utilities individually or in groups from third-party utility developers.

Several major utility packages are available for the PC. Each offers a battery of useful programs that enhance MS-DOS, boost performance in ways MS-DOS can't, or take the drudgery out of common computing tasks. This book concentrates on only four of the many packages available (but mentions others):

■ The Norton Utilities

■ PC Tools

■ The Mace Utilities

■ Checkit

The Norton Utilities were created by famed PC wizard Peter Norton. The original UnErase program was concocted by Norton. That, along with a disk "sector editor," formed the basis of the original Norton Utilities. Today the package comes with several dozen utilities, most of which are of the disk and data-recovery variety.

Central Point's PC Tools started out as a disk duplicator called Copy II PC. (The original Copy II Plus was for the old Apple II computer.) From that core utility grew a veritable kitchen sink of programs; today PC Tools consists of a dozen different utilities that perform tasks from PC communications to backup to data recovery. Also included is a handy MS-DOS shell program.

The Mace Utilities began as a disk-defragmentation utility—a novel idea at the time. It caught fire and made aviator Paul Mace into a software guru. The Mace Utilities still defragments disks; it also compacts files, safeguards data, and scans for viruses. These utilities have a nice "homebrew" feel to them.

Checkit is one of the leading PC diagnostic tools. It falls into the category of system analyses and diagnostics—one of many types of "What's in

Your PC" programs. Checkit can help you spot trouble, especially when it comes to finding bum RAM chips.

Rather than discuss each of these packages individually, the following sections deal with serious performance and maintenance problems and discusses those third-party utility packages that offer interesting solutions to each problem. Keep in mind that this isn't a tutorial and that the problems have no one solution. If you admire the way these products deal with the situation, you might want to consider investigating them further.

DELETED FILES

Almost every major utility has some sort of undelete command, but that command can operate on a variety of levels. For example, you can use MS-DOS's Undelete command with or without the Mirror command's deletion tracking. Without deletion tracking you can recover files, but with some extra effort. With deletion tracking, recovery is a cinch. Still, nothing is guaranteed; if a new file has invaded the deleted file's "space," recovery is impossible. Or is it?

PC Tools's Data Monitor

PC Tools's suite of programs includes special data-recovery utilities, one of which is the Data Monitor. It offers several interesting sub-features: Write Protection, which locks certain parts of a hard drive just as you would lock an entire floppy disk with a write-protect tab; Directory Lock, which encrypts files copied into specific subdirectories; a screen blanker; and Delete Sentry, which protects deleted files.

Delete Sentry has two modes of operation. The first mode works exactly like the Mirror command's deletion tracking under MS-DOS: It keeps a record of files you delete, allowing the Undelete command to effortlessly recover them. The second mode works like the "trash can" method of deleting files that I described in Chapter 3, but, as you would suspect, Delete Sentry is much more sophisticated.

For example, Delete Sentry monitors the Del command more carefully than Mirror does. Delete Sentry takes all the files you delete—or only the files matching wildcards you specify—and moves them to a hidden directory. The KILL.BAT program described in Chapter 3 works similarly, except that with Delete Sentry you move the files using the MS-DOS Del or Erase commands—you don't need to use Kill or any other non–MS-DOS command.

The "deleted" files sit in the secret directory awaiting possible recovery with PC Tools's Undelete command, which restores the files to their original drives and directories. Because the files aren't actually deleted, recovery with Delete Sentry is 100 percent—for a certain period of time. Delete Sentry allows you to set an automatic purge time for the files in the hidden directory, which keeps your hard disk from getting too full. Files that sit around longer than the specified number of days are then truly deleted.

Norton's Erase Protect

The Norton Utilities Erase Protect does virtually the same thing as PC Tools's Delete Sentry: It intercepts calls to delete files, moving the files instead to a secret directory named TRASHCAN off the root directory. Options and settings for Erase Protect are nearly identical to those for Delete Sentry.

Once you've configured Erase Protect, you run the program by entering *ep /on* at the MS-DOS prompt. You can monitor the status of deleted files by entering *ep /status*, and you can turn protection off by entering *ep /off*.

Files are plucked from Erase Protect's TRASHCAN directory using Norton's Unerase command. If you are using Norton Utilities, I recommend copying UNERASE.EXE into your MS-DOS subdirectory—or even renaming it UNDELETE.EXE, thereby replacing the MS-DOS external command.

DEFRAGMENTATION

The plague of fragmentation can be cured using MS-DOS by completely backing up and restoring a hard drive. But that's a lot of work to maintain a device that's supposed to make your life easier. If you want to defragment a drive but avoid backing up, you'll need to use a third-party utility.

When it comes to defragmenting drives, there are two ways to go: The first way is fast; the second way is thorough. Various utilities give you combinations of each.

To defragment a drive quickly, a program might simply relocate the files that are split into two or more pieces to a spot on disk where there's room for the whole thing. It might move other files out of the way, but if it doesn't need to, it won't. That's how the program gains its speed.

To defragment thoroughly, a program must relocate every file on the disk, picking them up and laying them end to end. (This is exactly what happens when you completely back up and restore the hard drive.) The thorough method "cures" the drive of fragmentation which, unlike the quick method, means you won't need to rerun the program as often.

In either case, you should defragment a drive only when fragmentation affects about 10 percent or more of its files. (Many defragmentation utilities tell you the percentage of affected files before they begin.) And you won't see an obvious performance improvement unless you're defragmenting a hard drive with 50 percent or more fragmented files.

The first real defragmentation utility became available with early versions of the Mace Utilities. At the time, many hard drives were terribly fragmented, and the performance boost Mace offered was enough to spread the program's reputation by word of mouth. Today, the defragmentation utility is still the Mace cornerstone, supplemented by diagnostic tools that tell you if your drive needs defragmenting.

Other popular disk-defragmentation utilities include PC Tools's Compress, Norton's Speed Disk, and Golden Bow's VOpt. They all do the job—some faster than others and some more thoroughly than others.

Defragmentation utilities move a lot of files around and constantly update the FAT. When using one of these utilities, my advice is to back up before you begin and reset after you're done. Backing up protects you against any power outages that might occur while you're defragmenting. If the power goes, files might be lost or corrupted. You can run Chkdsk to clean up the mess, but it's better to simply restore from your backup disks should the power go out. To ensure that MS-DOS reads the new FAT, always reset when you're done defragmenting—even if the utility claims that you don't need to.

DISK TUNE-UPS

Disk tune-up utilities do a variety of things for grouchy hard drives, most of which relate to the low-level format. That sounds scary because the low-level format isn't something you want to mess with. But, instead of wiping out a disk, these programs can work with the low-level format in a nondestructive and beneficial way.

Many disk tune-up utilities start out by performing a battery of tests and displaying results along with suggestions for improvements. For example, one suggestion might be to change the disk's interleave factor. Normally you can make this change only with a destructive low-level reformat of the hard drive. However, because the tune-up program can perform a low-level reformat without erasing any data, the result is improved performance without data loss.

In the realm of preventive maintenance, some disk tune-up programs perform a *surface scan* of your hard disk. The surface-scan routine reads and writes "test patterns" to every disk sector, checking for any errors. Again, no data is lost. If the routine finds a bad sector, it moves the data in that sector elsewhere and marks the sector as bad in the FAT. This maintenence procedure helps avoid future problems with the disk.

Finally, there's a pinch of alchemy in some of these programs, which claim to revitalize your disk by reading and writing every sector. This supposedly "wakes up" the magnetic particles and can bring back disks from the brink of extinction. I seriously question the validity of this claim, but if you're a believer, go ahead and run these programs.

The following sections describe two utilities that perform various types of disk tune-up. These are technical programs—not to be taken lightly. As usual, back up before you use any utility that messes with the hard drive.

Norton's Calibrate

You use the Norton Utilities' Calibrate program to diagnose and remedy disk problems related to the low-level format. The program performs several tests before the actual calibration, using interactive histograms to graphically suggest ways of boosting your hard disk's performance. You can actually see how the disk's performance will change under certain circumstances. If you select an option based on the results of the test, Calibrate reformats the disk accordingly.

With some drives—specifically, IDE and SCSI drives—reformatting at a low level isn't possible, so Calibrate simply reports statistics for those drives. However, even with those drives you can use Calibrate to perform a surface scan that checks for questionable sectors and rescues any data from bad parts of the disk.

PC Tools's DiskFix

PC Tools's DiskFix is a multipurpose program that does both disk tune-up and repair. For disk tune-ups, you can select DiskFix's Surface Scan and Revitalize options from its main menu.

Surface Scan uses pattern testing to locate bad sectors on the disk. If it finds any, the program moves the data in those sectors elsewhere and ropes off the sectors, marking them as bad.

Revitalize performs a battery of tests on the disk, checking various aspects of its performance. After the tests are done, the program displays a histogram of the results. You can select a new low-level format or interleave from the histogram, and Revitalize then reformats your disk to those specifications.

GENERAL REPAIR

The category of general repair includes utilities that diagnose and attempt to fix major disk ailments. Some of these utilities are simply combinations of programs already covered in this book. For example, a general repair utility might use the Mirror command to "automatically" repair a downed hard drive. However, other utilities offer clever solutions for reviving downed hard drives and getting your data back.

Generally, these programs start by diagnosing the problem: Can the drive boot? Is the partition table good? Is the boot sector good? Then they go into extensive analysis of the FAT, checking for unused clusters and cross-linked files. Finally, they analyze the directory structure and all the files on the disk. All anomalies are fixed as the program encounters them.

In a way, these programs are magic: They can repair some hopeless situations and give you back your system. For example, whereas Chkdsk reports cross-linked sectors and does nothing about them, a general repair utility identifies and resolves cross-linked sectors, giving you your files back.

Although these utilities can solve problems and restore data, you should consider the nature of disk problems in general. Miracles aside, major problems with your hard disk usually indicate some type of hardware failure. Especially if the problems reoccur, consider getting a new hard drive as opposed to running some disk-repair utility on a regular basis.

One additional warning: As with the disk tune-up utilities, general repair utilities might not work with all hard drives or all versions of MS-DOS. Check each utility's manual about incompatibilities before you launch into anything.

Each of the three major utility packages has its own general repair utility: PC Tools has DiskFix, the Mace Utilities has Emergency Room, and Norton has Disk Doctor. If you have one of these programs, consider copying it to your Emergency Boot Disk as a possible aid in future disk repair.

DIAGNOSTIC TOOLS

Diagnostic utility programs perform two functions:

■ They give you an accurate summary of your computer system, including detailed information about its memory, hard drive, and interrupt (IRQ) assignments, and sundry other information.

■ They troubleshoot the system, offering suggestions for improving performance, resolving conflicts, and locating defective RAM chips (a real time-saver).

System Information

A common type of diagnostic program is the *system info* program, which provides a summary of your system and might perform some speed, or "benchmark," tests. PC Tools and the Norton Utilities come with system info programs (SI.EXE for PC Tools and SYSINFO.EXE for Norton).

Quarterdeck Office Systems offers Manifest, a specialized system info program that provides a summary of your system but with a concentration on memory management. Unlike the Norton and PC Tools system info programs, Manifest provides no system-wide benchmarks. However, it does offer "hints" on how to improve your PC's memory—which usually involve buying other Quarterdeck products.

Ashton-Tate/Borland sells a product called Control Room that offers features similar to the other programs mentioned in this section.

These programs aren't well-suited to resolving any problems or performing extensive diagnostics. What they're good at is telling you what's in your PC, and that can aid in the troubleshooting process.

TouchStone Software's Checkit

Checkit is an example of a system info program that also provides diagnostics. It works similarly to the standard system info utilities, but it also compares your PC's statistics with values it knows apply to well-behaved computers. When a difference crops up, Checkit alerts you to the potential problem. So while it doesn't actually fix the problem, it will tell you where it's located.

Checkit has a whole battery of tests it can perform on just about any PC. It can test memory, the disk drives, the motherboard, the clock, the serial and printer ports, the printer itself, the video display, the keyboard, the mouse, and the joystick. It's quite thorough.

The tests help you evaluate your PC. Beyond that, Checkit comes with special tools, one of which will locate bad RAM chips. This can be invaluable when you've installed a bank of RAM chips and one of the chips is reported as bad. Checkit tells you exactly where that bad chip is located.

Your Own Diagnostic Program

Almost every PC comes with its own diagnostic disk. Some of these are fairly sophisticated, and that usually depends on who made your PC. (Some PC manufacturers include a copy of Checkit with their computers.)

Most PC diagnostic programs come on their own bootable disks. They have the advantage of being keyed to your own personal computer, so they're very precise when compared with general diagnostic programs. On the downside, often they'll analyze only your manufacturer's brand-name peripherals. For example, Dell's analyzer locates only a Dell mouse—not the standard Microsoft mouse.

As part of the troubleshooting process, a diagnostic disk can be invaluable. If you lack one, create a custom one using the *format /s* command and then copying a system info or diagnostic program to that disk. Properly label the disk and keep it handy with your Emergency Boot Disk for possible future use.

SUMMARY

Where MS-DOS ends, third-party utilities begin. Many of these utilities offer the same tools MS-DOS has, but with extra flash. Some of the utilities that go beyond what MS-DOS offers are necessary: Hard-disk optimization programs are highly recommended, though it's up to you to choose which package you want.

Generally speaking, beware of feature battles. There's no sense in paying for a lot of things you don't need. Stick to the basics. You now know how your system works, how to make it work better, and what you can do should something go wrong. Put that knowledge to work, and if you need a third-party utility, select one based on your needs.

Chapter 11
Troubleshooting Guide

This chapter offers general troubleshooting information for common PC problems. Most errors and system glitches are easily fixed once you recognize them. In this chapter, you'll read about how to locate those errors and glitches, and you'll learn how to anticipate and deal with other potential problems. Everything is done using MS-DOS, although where appropriate, third-party utilities arc also mentioned.

SIGNS AND SYMPTOMS

Troubleshooting involves two steps: First, you diagnose the problem; second, you fix it. MS-DOS helps you diagnose most problems, primarily through its crror messages. The Chkdsk utility also alerts you to potential trouble. When you find the problem, you can attempt to fix it using the MS-DOS file tools.

Your first troubleshooting step is to determine whether you have a hardware problem or a software problem. Software problems can generally be fixed using MS-DOS or some specialized utility. Hardware problems, however, are another animal.

If you suspect hardware trouble, refer to the first section of Chapter 7 and review the questions to determine whether the problem is hardware-related. The most important thing to ascertain is whether the problem is consistent across all applications. If the problem does not occur across all applications, or if the problem is reported by Chkdsk or exists with only one file, continue reading here.

GENERAL SUGGESTIONS

Before you set out to discover what's wrong with your system, keep the following points in mind.

Back Up!

Nothing beats a recent backup. However, knowing when to back up is important. Suppose you suspect trouble and decide to do a full hard-disk drive backup. Back up to a *new* disk set, just in case. That way, if any problems are carried over in the backup, you'll have your older backup disk sets as double insurance. (A similar argument can be made for having two copies of the MIRROR.FIL file: you have one for backup purposes in case the first copy becomes corrupted.)

Always Make One Change at a Time

It's easier to detect problems when you change or modify your system one step at a time. Specifically, never alter CONFIG.SYS or AUTOEXEC.BAT without verifying that each change works. It's easier to nail down a problem that's related to the change you've just made as opposed to untangling a snarl of seven recent changes.

Reboot to Test the System

After changing CONFIG.SYS or AUTOEXEC.BAT, reset to be sure everything still works. Resetting is also a good response to quirks that occur in the system. For example, if MS-DOS suddenly forgets about your floppy-disk drive, or if a program runs amok, resetting might help. (Always remember to exit all applications or environments, such as Microsoft Windows, before resetting.)

Keep a Boot Disk Handy

Keep a boot disk, such as the Emergency Boot Disk, handy. If your hard-disk drive suddenly flakes out, you'll need a boot disk to bring up your system for troubleshooting.

Troubleshoot Before You Call Technical Support

Try to figure out the problem on your own before you cash in your tech-support chips. True, some places offer toll-free "800" technical support, but don't take unfair advantage of it. Don't call until you've tried to troubleshoot the problem on your own. (The technician will appreciate that you've gone the extra mile.) And be sure to have all the necessary information ready when you do call.

THE MS-DOS TROUBLESHOOTER: CHKDSK

Chkdsk is the best MS-DOS tool for troubleshooting. Even third-party utilities have you run Chkdsk to test for cross-linked files, lost clusters, and bad FATs. But keep in mind that Chkdsk isn't a miracle worker. In fact, it does a lot less than what most users think.

Chkdsk stands for Check Disk, although a more accurate name might be Check FAT. What Chkdsk does is to "walk through" your FAT, ensuring that every file in every directory has proper FAT entries. If any FAT entry exists without having a matching file in a directory, it is reported as a "lost chain" or "lost allocation unit" and optionally converted by Chkdsk into a file in the root directory. And if a file exists in a directory without having a matching FAT entry, you'll see a "file truncated" error message as Chkdsk tries to match the file to a proper allocation unit in the FAT.

Chkdsk ends its duties by reading in key values about the disk from its boot sector. Then it reports a summary of the disk's size, bytes free and used, and other miscellaneous information. It's all really trivia, though— Chkdsk simply reports information already stored on the disk, not the results of any tests it makes itself.

Chkdsk does *not* physically analyze the disk for bad sectors. If it reports any bad sectors, they're simply marked that way in the FAT by the Format command when it originally verified the disk. If any additional bad sectors crop up, or if the disk is physically damaged, Chkdsk cannot detect the problem and reports nothing.

Performing a Regular Disk Check

Periodically run the Chkdsk command on each of your hard-disk drives. Always specify the /F switch, as in *chkdsk /f*, which directs Chkdsk to convert any lost chains to files. The files will be named FILE0000.CHK through FILE9999.CHK, one for each lost chain recovered. When Chkdsk is done, delete these files from the drive's root directory:

```
C>del \file*.chk
```

In the example, \FILE*.CHK matches any files Chkdsk creates. This might seem odd, because Chkdsk is supposed to "rescue" those lost chains. In practice, however, most lost chains contain garbage. You can view the files using the Type command, but odds are if you find anything worth keeping it's probably stowed safely in some other file already on disk.

Note that you should not use Chkdsk when files are open on the disk. Don't run Chkdsk when memory-resident programs might have files open (such as a pop-up text editor), when shelling out of a program where files might be open, or when running Windows, the MS-DOS Shell, or some other multiprogram environment.

Using Chkdsk for Troubleshooting

Chkdsk can report a variety of errors, most of which will tell you that some form of troubleshooting is in order. Chkdsk will repair any files, directories, or the FAT as best it can—if you specify the /F switch! If the problem persists, however, you should attempt to rescue your files out of questionable directories: Copy the files to a new directory and delete the originals. Then remove the suspect directory. If Chkdsk reports a problem with the FAT, the only solution is to back up the disk as best you can and then reformat the disk.

Note: If you back up your disk due to a Chkdsk error, use a new backup disk set. You want to be sure that other recent backups remain intact. After reformatting the disk, try to restore from the most recent backup. If the problem persists, reformat again and then restore from the next most recent backup.

Error Messages

Chkdsk's troubleshooting error messages are listed here, along with suggestions for fixing the associated problem. Third-party solutions are discussed later.

Cannot CHDIR to xxx/root

Cause: Chkdsk tried to change to a named directory and couldn't. This error is okay if the directory is a Subst'd or Join'd directory; Chkdsk displays *tree past this point not processed* and continues as normal. However, if the directory is the root directory, you have a problem.

Solution: If Chkdsk cannot change to the root directory, reset your computer. Then check the root directory of the drive. If the directory is corrupted or if Chkdsk still reports the error, back up your disk as best you can. Reformat the drive. Note that using Mirror or the Unformat command at this point will simply copy back a corrupted root directory; your best choice is to reformat and hope you have a recent backup disk handy.

Cannot recover ../. entry

Cause: A subdirectory's . (dot) or .. (dot-dot) entry is incorrect. Chkdsk tried to fix the problem but could not.

Solution: Try to copy the files in that subdirectory elsewhere. Use *xcopy* /s to copy all files to another directory on disk and then delete the original files. Remove the original, corrupted directory using the Rd command.

Directory is totally empty, no . or ..

Cause: The subdirectory does not contain the . (dot) or .. (dot-dot) directory entries. Chkdsk cannot check files or subdirectories from that point on in the tree.

Solution: Try using *chkdsk* /f to repair the damage. If the problem persists, copy the files from the subdirectory and delete the originals; remove the questionable subdirectory.

Disk error reading/writing FAT xxx

Cause: Chkdsk could not access the FAT. This can happen if the sectors where the FAT is located are damaged.

Solution: Try using *chkdsk* /f. If that doesn't solve the problem, the disk sectors are bad. Back up the disk and reformat the drive.

Does not exist

This is the same error as *Directory is totally empty, no . or ..*, which is described above.

Entry has a bad attribute/size/link

Cause: The . (dot) or .. (dot-dot) directory entries contain bad information about their attributes, size, or links. (This is actually three different error messages.)

Solution: Use *chkdsk* /f.

File allocation table bad, drive *X*

Cause: There is an error in the FAT in drive *X*.

Solution: Try using *chkdsk /f* to repair the FAT. If this doesn't work, back up and reformat the drive.

Invalid sub-directory entry

Cause: It's the old . (dot) or .. (dot-dot) directory entries again. They contain erroneous information that Chkdsk has detected.

Solution: If *chkdsk /f* doesn't resolve the problem, try moving files out of the directory and then deleting that directory with Rd.

Is cross linked on allocation unit *xxx*

Cause: Chkdsk has discovered that two files are sharing the same disk cluster; both are claiming ownership of a single part of the FAT. This is about the scariest Chkdsk message.

Solution: Copy one of the files to another location on disk, and then delete the original file. Then use *chkdsk /f* to verify that everything's okay. Also check the file to be sure it's fully intact; one of the two cross-linked files probably contains invalid information.

If the cross-linked file was a directory, move all files from that directory to another directory on disk. Remove the cross-linked directory using the Rd command.

Unrecoverable error in directory
Convert directory to file (Y/N)?

Cause: Chkdsk has tried to fix the directory but failed.

Solution: You're asked whether you want to convert the directory into a file on disk. Try pressing N first. Return to MS-DOS and rescue as many files as possible from the directory and then delete the directory.

If you press Y, MS-DOS turns the directory into a file, which is probably not what you want. Use *chkdsk /f* again to try to recover some files—but don't delete them from your root directory! Check each one to see if it contains any valuable information. (A utility program like Lotus Magellan would help here, or any program that views files "in context.") There's nothing you can do with the directory "file," so delete it.

Third-Party Utilities

Third-party utilities can do more than the MS-DOS simple "move the files and delete the directory" instructions. First, third-party utilities always try to resolve conflicts without your having to delete anything. Second, these programs can patch up the FAT and give you access to directories and files that MS-DOS assumes are long gone.

Both PC Tools's DiskFix and the Norton Utilities' Disk Doctor attempt to rescue lost files, directories, and FATs without destroying anything. Sometimes the solutions are complex, forcing you to "walk through" various recovery steps. If your data is important, follow the instructions carefully and you might get it back.

Above all, be aware that disk problems and glitches might be hints of hardware failure. For example, cross-linked files usually occur when a hard disk's controller is failing (or when you're running a questionable disk utility). If disk problems persist, your hardware might be telling you that it needs to be replaced.

PROBLEMS AND SOLUTIONS

Running Chkdsk or third-party diagnostic programs will help you uncover and repair some types of disk errors, specifically FAT errors. If you experience trouble starting your computer, problems with disks and files, or just general weirdness, the following sections will help you troubleshoot.

One general bit of good advice: A great portion of successful recovery depends upon using the Mirror command to create a system-area image file, MIRROR.FIL. Refer to Chapter 6 for more information about Mirror.

Booting and Startup Problems

When your system first starts, it performs a *power-on self test*, or POST. Additionally, some parts of your system, such as the video adapter, hard-disk drive, and network BIOS, will also perform their own POSTs. These diagnostic tests will alert you to any potential hardware problems. (If something odd happens, refer to "Problem Hunting" in Chapter 7.) After that, it's the software that boots your system.

Non-DOS or boot disk

When the hard-disk drive doesn't come up, start the system from your Emergency Boot Disk. Then if you can change to the hard-disk drive, that means it's okay—but that it's not a boot disk. Transfer the system files to the hard-disk drive using the *sys c:* command, reset, and try again.

If "Sys'ing" the drive fails, you might have a corrupted root directory. Try the Unformat command to restore the root directory and boot information (if you've run the Mirror command on your drive). If this doesn't work, reformat the drive and restore all your files from a backup disk set.

Bad partition table

You can recover a partition table using the *unformat /partn* command, as described in Chapter 8. If you don't have the PARTNSAV.FIL file the Mirror command creates, you can manually reconstruct the partition table. The Norton Utilities' Disk Doctor describes a painstaking way to do this.

Bad boot sector

You can recover a drive's boot sector using the Unformat command along with the MIRROR.FIL file created by the Mirror command. Use the *sys c:* command to rebuild the boot sector on a hard drive. However, if the boot sector is damaged, you must reformat the drive.

Bad or missing Command Interpreter

This means that COMMAND.COM (the command interpreter) cannot be found. You need a copy of COMMAND.COM in the root directory of a boot disk. If the Sys command didn't copy it there (as was the case with older versions of MS-DOS), reset using the Emergency Boot Disk and copy COMMAND.COM to your hard disk's root directory.

This problem also crops up when the Shell configuration command is used. Shell is used to indicate the location of a command processor not in the root directory; for example, *shell=c:\dos\command.com*. Be sure that COMMAND.COM is in that directory and that you've specified the name correctly. (My advice is to keep COMMAND.COM in the root directory and dispense with the Shell command.)

COMMAND not found/
Cannot load COMMAND, system halted

This message occurs sometimes after quitting a program. The location for the COMMAND.COM file is stored in the MS-DOS environment using the COMSPEC variable. If the COMSPEC variable indicates an incorrect location for COMMAND.COM, MS-DOS cannot load the command interpreter after you quit a program. Check to see that COMSPEC is set properly. Enter *set* at the MS-DOS prompt and look for a line that reads similar to the following:

```
comspec=c:\command.com
```

If you have booted from a floppy-disk drive, MS-DOS will look for the COMMAND.COM file there. If you have put the COMMAND.COM file elsewhere using the Shell configuration command, that location will be reflected.

You can reset COMSPEC using the Set command. For example:

```
C>set comspec=c:\command.com
```

Add this to AUTOEXEC.BAT if it's a persistent problem, carefully specifying the proper location for COMMAND.COM. (In this example, the root directory is assumed.)

Note: Do not copy COMMAND.COM to a RAM drive and specify that location using the COMSPEC variable. Any program that corrupts your RAM drive will likely corrupt that copy of COMMAND.COM and cause the system to halt.

Cannot find system files

MS-DOS cannot boot the disk because the boot files aren't on it. Reset using a bootable disk, such as the Emergency Boot Disk. Use the Sys command to copy the boot files to the non-booting disk. For example, enter *sys c:*, which will make the hard-disk drive a boot disk.

Disk Problems

Chapter 3 discussed many of the problems associated with floppy disks. The most annoying problems occur when you format low-capacity disks to high capacity—or vice-versa. This can result in the *Bad Disk/Unreadable*

Track 0 error message, which is addressed specifically in Chapter 3, in "Dealing with Unreadable Disks." Other crises are discussed here.

Cannot log to drive

Drives can go "off line" for a number of reasons. Typically, when a program corrupts the MS-DOS drive tables, you'll notice missing drives. Immediately quit any application and reset your computer. This will rebuild the drive tables and get your system back on line.

Some external drives might be set up using special device drivers. Be sure they're properly installed in CONFIG.SYS and that other installation programs haven't stomped all over them (juggled them around or "REM'd" them out). Note that hard-disk device drivers, such as SCSI drivers, appear *first* in your CONFIG.SYS file.

Abort, Retry, Ignore, Fail?

The classic MS-DOS "tossing-in-the-towel" error message displays the prompt "Abort, Retry, Ignore" with the deadly "Fail" question being added on occasion. Press the first letter of the appropriate word to select it: A for Abort, R for Retry, and so on.

MS-DOS displays this message only after it's tried a disk (or device) read or write operation several times. Basically, MS-DOS has tried its best to get something done, and it has failed. It needs your input to decide which course to take. These are the consequences of each option:

Abort MS-DOS cancels the program—if it can. If you're running an MS-DOS program or utility (such as Copy or Format), this is the same as pressing Ctrl+C to cancel.

Retry MS-DOS attempts to do the same thing over again. If it fails again, the same prompt will appear. This should be your first choice.

Ignore MS-DOS returns to the program with the message "operation successful!" regardless of the outcome. This is not a good idea. Don't select this option.

Fail MS-DOS returns to the program with an error message reflecting the problem. If the program can handle the problem, okay. If not, the program might proceed assuming nothing is wrong. Select this option rarely.

The most common *Abort, Retry, Ignore* error message occurs when a floppy disk is missing in drive A or B. You'll see: *Not ready reading drive A*. To solve the problem, insert a disk in the drive and press R for Retry. (It helps to have a few formatted disks lying about just in case you unwittingly log to an empty floppy-disk drive.)

Here is a list of error messages you'll often see hovering above the *Abort, Retry, Ignore* prompt:

```
Error reading/writing hard/fixed disk

General failure

Not ready

Read fault error

Sector not found

Seek error
```

For most of these, press R a few times to see if the operation meets with success. If not, press A. A diagnostics check of the drive might be in order to make sure it's up to snuff. You might also see this message:

```
Write protect error
```

This message means that the disk is write-protected. It was made that way for a reason; someone didn't want you changing files or writing to the disk. You can manually remove the write protection by sliding the tile on a 3½-inch disk or by peeling off the write-protect tab on a 5¼-inch disk.

This message might also appear on a hard-disk drive. Don't panic. An old utility, LOCK.COM, was designed to fool MS-DOS into thinking the hard-disk drive was write-protected. If you aren't running such a program and the hard-disk drive still reports that it's write-protected, resetting should clear up the problem.

Troubleshooting CONFIG.SYS and AUTOEXEC.BAT

Make changes to CONFIG.SYS or AUTOEXEC.BAT one line at a time. Test your system after each change to help track down bugs. You can also create a boot disk, copy CONFIG.SYS and AUTOEXEC.BAT to it, and then make your changes there instead. When everything checks out, copy the files back to the hard-disk drive, reset, and test one final time.

The most common problems in CONFIG.SYS are misspellings. You'll see one of the two CONFIG.SYS-specific error messages:

```
Unrecognized command in CONFIG.SYS

Error in CONFIG.SYS line xxx
```

These messages help you locate bad configuration commands or misleading Device commands. Also, be aware of any device drivers you might have moved to other subdirectories when "housekeeping"; remember to update their locations in CONFIG.SYS.

Troubleshooting AUTOEXEC.BAT is the same as troubleshooting any other batch file. If you see the message *Syntax error*, you've probably goofed up some batch-file command. Remember that the If-equal comparison test requires *two* equal signs. Also, the For command has been known to wreak havoc. Refer to your MS-DOS manual for the proper format.

If the problem is a *Bad command or file name* error message, you'll have to do some work to track it down. Start by reviewing AUTOEXEC.BAT in your text editor. Check one line at a time, looking for misspellings and inaccurately listed subdirectories. If this fails, edit the initial *echo off* to read *echo on*, reset, and watch the batch file as it runs. (You might need to add some Pause commands to slow down the listing, or REM out some Cls commands.) Save any changes you make to your CONFIG.SYS or AUTOEXEC.BAT file, and remember to reset to test things out.

File Trouble

The best advice for avoiding file irregularity is to follow the tips on file management provided in Chapter 2. But when you smell the foul brew of failure, this advice should help.

Finding a Lost File

Is the file lost or are you? Use the Cd command to be sure you're in the proper directory. Some programs work like a city bus: They pick you up in one subdirectory and drop you off in another. Many times I've created a file that I believed to be in one directory but that the application placed into another directory.

After you have looked everywhere, try the following command to locate a lost file:

dir *filename* /s

Replace *filename* with the name of the file you're looking for. MS-DOS will scan the entire hard-disk drive, starting with the root directory, for any filenames that match. When it's found, the file will appear in the following format:

```
Directory of C:\LOST\BOPEEP

SHEEP    TXT      2033 06-08-92  12:10p
         1 file(s)          2033 bytes
```

The file SHEEP.TXT was found in the BOPEEP directory.

If you see the message *File not found*, try the command again using wildcards. Or you might want to try the same command on another hard-disk drive.

Bad Commands or Filenames

The message *Bad command or file name* is the universal response when MS-DOS doesn't understand what you've typed at the prompt. If you didn't make a typing error, the program you want to run isn't in the current directory and MS-DOS hasn't found it on the search path.

First check your directory with the Cd command. Then check the path using the Path command; some program or batch file might have changed the path—or the search path could have been overwritten when something else was added to an already full environment.

If you still cannot locate the program, use the same command as described earlier for locating a file. For example:

dir *p rogram.** /s

Replace *program* with the name of the program you want to run. The asterisk wildcard will match any extension, including COM, EXE, or BAT. Note the location of the file when found, and then use Cd to move to that directory and run the program.

Beware of Hidden Files

Hidden files can really goof you up. They are especially sticky when you are trying to remove a directory and keep getting the message *directory not empty*. To display only hidden files in the current directory, use the following command:

```
C>dir /a:h
```

A *File not found* message shows no hidden files. Otherwise you'll see only those files invisible to the regular Dir command (and Copy, Del, and so on). To strip the files of their hidden attribute, use the Attrib command:

attrib -h *filename*

The -H switch removes the hidden attribute from the file *filename*. You can use wildcards to specify groups of files. (In addition, you can use the UNHIDE batch file described in Chapter 6.)

Unable to Create a File

There are two reasons you cannot create a file: The disk or directory is full, or creating a file would overwrite a file that has special protection, such as a directory or read-only file.

Disks can be filled with files, in which case you'll see a *Disk full* error message. But don't be misled: It's possible to fill up a disk simply by putting too many files in the root directory. If you have 512 files in the root directory of any hard-disk drive—no matter how many megabytes of space are still available—MS-DOS tells you the disk is full, and no new files can be added. To solve the problem, copy one of the files to a floppy disk. In its place, create a subdirectory—for example, BLOAT—and then copy *all* of the files from the root directory to that new subdirectory with the command *xcopy *.* \bloat*. Finally, copy from the floppy disk to the BLOAT directory the file you moved.

To clean up the root directory, delete all files except COMMAND.COM, CONFIG.SYS, AUTOEXEC.BAT, and anything else that positively must be in the root directory. Finally, read "Organizing Your Hard Disk" in Chapter 2.

The second situation in which you cannot create a file is when a file or directory of the same name already exists in the directory. In the case of a directory, it's impossible for MS-DOS to overwrite it with a new file; choose a new name for the file you want to create.

Normally files can be overwritten—often unexpectedly by the MS-DOS Copy command—unless they have their read-only attributes set. (You can remove a file's read-only status with *attrib -r*. More about that in a moment.) However, I recommend selecting a new name for the file you want to create; files are made read-only for a reason.

Removing Files That Won't Die

The infamous zombie files just won't go away! If you see the message *Access denied*, remove the file's read-only protection using Attrib:

attrib -r *filename*

If the file still won't go away, you probably have a disk error, or damage has been done to the directory. Try using *chkdsk /f*. Afterward, copy all files and subdirectories from that directory to another location and then remove the directory. If this doesn't work, you might need a third-party utility to examine the disk.

COMMANDS TO AVOID

Four MS-DOS commands—Append, Ctty, Recover, and Setver—when misused, can lead to a world of trouble. Each of these commands has a purpose, but they can lead to trouble if you're not careful.

The following sections describe each of these commands, along with information on how to recover if they're accidentally used.

Append

The Append command allows MS-DOS to locate data files in a special search path or in the standard MS-DOS program search path. At first this sounds great: Just as MS-DOS can locate programs in directories other than the current one, it can also locate data files. In practice, however, this can be disastrous.

Basically, Append was created to satisfy those people who wanted access to remote files without having to learn their disk's directory structure. The risk comes when you delete files; the Del command searches through directories quickly and efficiently. Del *.* can be devastating, deleting hundreds of files across several directories!

It's better to work with your hard-disk drive's structure and organization instead of relying on half solutions like Append. If you use the command and understand it, that's great. Otherwise, it's not recommended.

Ctty

With the Ctty command, you can define a device for MS-DOS standard input and output. Normally this is set to CON, or the console device; input comes from the keyboard and output is displayed on the screen. Using Ctty, you can specify another MS-DOS device instead of CON.

The most common device used with Ctty is the serial port, or COM*x* device. For example, you can connect a laptop or some other PC to your system using a direct-connect cable, configure the MS-DOS serial port using the Mode command, and enter *ctty com1*. MS-DOS then expects all input from and sends all output to the COM1 device. Essentially, you can use the remote computer to control your PC. This sounds handy, but it's really quite limited. Only MS-DOS and those programs that use its I/O will work; everything else still comes up on the local computer. You cannot use Ctty to send files back and forth.

You can also use the Ctty command to shut off console input while a batch file runs. For example, a batch-file programmer might put *ctty nul* at the start of the batch file, cutting off all input and output. The command *ctty con* is required at the end of the batch file to give control back to the user.

Ctty can be handy. But without the proper *ctty con* command, you'll never get back control of your computer. (And with some other device in control, it makes typing "ctty con" all the more difficult.) This is nothing a hard reset won't fix, but using Ctty is not worth the potential trouble in most cases.

Recover

The Recover command has a promising name but can be deadly. In fact, the *Norton Troubleshooting Guide* recommends that you delete the RECOVER.EXE program from your hard drive—immediately!

The Recover command attempts to fix files that happen to be lying across bad sectors on disk. For example, suppose a file sits across several sectors and one of the sectors is bad. The Recover command will convert it into a new file, FILE0000.REC, containing the intact sectors plus as much of the damaged sector as possible. For text files, that's great. For a spreadsheet or some other intricate data file, the results would be questionable.

On the catastrophic side, if you use the Recover command without an optional filename, it will convert *everything* on the current disk—whether it needs fixing or not—into a recover file. This includes subdirectories, which means *recover c:* will totally zap the subdirectory structure of your hard-disk drive.

However, there is life after accidentally using the Recover command. Basically, Recover changes only the root directory of a disk; the FAT and boot sector are still 100 percent okay, as are all the files on your disk. If you've used the Mirror command recently on the disk, recovery is possible using the Unformat command. Without Mirror, you're stuck.

Even if you feel the need to run the Recover command, don't. It does display the following warning, giving you ample time to back out:

```
The entire drive will be reconstructed,
directory structures will be destroyed.
Are you sure (Y/N)?
```

Don't press Y! Instead of Recover, I recommend using a third-party file-recovery utility.

Setver

The Setver command is a useful and positive MS-DOS command. But it's sneaky, which can have a negative effect under some circumstances.

Setver fools a program into thinking it's running under a specific version of MS-DOS—specifically a version other than MS-DOS 5. Setver came about because some programs were incompatible with various versions of MS-DOS, typically MS-DOS 1.0. Programmers would write a routine into an application to check if a certain MS-DOS version was being used. If the specified version was not used, the program wouldn't run. To make programs compatible with MS-DOS 5, Setver tells MS-DOS 5 to pretend it's some earlier version of MS-DOS.

If you don't have any programs that require Setver, or you never see an *Incompatible DOS version* type of error message, you don't need to install Setver. Installing Setver might be counterproductive in some cases. For example, I have an old program that would run only with MS-DOS 3.2. When I tricked the program into thinking MS-DOS 5 was really 3.2, my entire system crashed. Upgrade your software to versions compatible with MS-DOS 5. Then you can dispense with Setver.

SUMMARY

Troubleshooting involves identifying problems and then dealing with them. With MS-DOS, this means reading and understanding error messages and then being able to remedy the situation as best as possible.

The major MS-DOS troubleshooting commands are Mirror and Chkdsk. Mirror is used to create the MIRROR.FIL file, which will help you recover root-directory errors. Chkdsk can diagnose and remedy FAT problems, directory problems, and cross-linked files. If the problems aren't resolved, you can back up or copy programs from questionable subdirectories and then delete those subdirectories.

Third-party utilities offer more thorough methods of disk repair. However, you want to recover important data without causing a major interruption in your computing schedule. Some third-party solutions are quite technical, beyond the abilities of the common PC user.

Finally, keep in mind that frequent disk problems could be an indication of hardware failure. Don't ignore the warnings a failing hard-disk drive makes before it's too late!

Appendix A

Computer Stat Sheet

Fill in the information on this sheet and keep it or a photocopy of it with your computer's manual. Use this information for troubleshooting or when talking with technical-support people about a problem.

SYSTEM

Enter the name of your system, type of CPU and speed, and whether or not a math coprocessor is installed and what type it is.

System name: _____

CPU:

☐ 8088/8086   ☐ 80286   ☐ 386SX

☐ 80386   ☐ 80486   ☐ Other: _____

Speed: ____ MHz   Math coprocessor? ☐ No ☐ Yes: _____

MEMORY

Identify the amount of memory in various parts of your computer. Remember to specify the value as KB (kilobytes) or MB (megabytes). Use the Mem command to get this information.

Conventional memory: _____   Extended memory: _____

Expanded memory: _____

DISK DRIVES

Fill in the information on the next page about your floppy-disk drives, their physical size, and capacity in kilobytes or megabytes.

Floppy drive A: ☐ 5¼-inch   ☐ 3½-inch   Capacity: _____

Floppy drive B: ☐ 5¼-inch   ☐ 3½-inch   Capacity: _____

Additional floppy drives: ☐ 5¼-inch   ☐ 3½-inch   Capacity: _____

For each hard-disk drive, indicate the total size of the drive in megabytes. Hard disk 0 is your first hard-disk drive. Further, indicate the size of each partition, if applicable. Select option 4 from the Fdisk command's main menu to determine these values.

Hard disk 0:   Total size: _____

   Drive letter: ____ Size: _____   Drive letter: ____ Size:_____

   Drive letter: ____ Size: _____   Drive letter: ____ Size:_____

   Drive letter: ____ Size: _____   Drive letter: ____ Size:_____

Hard disk 1:   Total size: _____

   Drive letter: ____ Size: _____   Drive letter: ____ Size:_____

   Drive letter: ____ Size: _____   Drive letter: ____ Size:_____

Additional hard disks:

   Drive letter: ____ Size: _____   Drive letter: ____ Size:_____

   Drive letter: ____ Size: _____   Drive letter: ____ Size:_____

VIDEO

Identify the type of video system you have in your PC. The standard adapter types are listed below. For VGA cards, be sure to enter the amount of memory on the card.

Type:

   ☐ Monochrome MDA   ☐ Hercules   ☐ CGA

   ☐ EGA   ☐ VGA   ☐ SuperVGA

   ☐ Other: _____   VGA Memory: _____

PORTS

Mark "No" or "Yes" if your system is equipped with the following ports. If "Yes," indicate the type of device connected to the port.

Printer LPT1: ☐ No ☐ Yes _____

Printer LPT2: ☐ No ☐ Yes _____

Printer LPT3: ☐ No ☐ Yes _____

Serial COM1: ☐ No ☐ Yes _____

Serial COM2: ☐ No ☐ Yes _____

Serial COM3: ☐ No ☐ Yes _____

Serial COM4: ☐ No ☐ Yes _____

EXPANSION CARDS

Enter the type of expansion card installed in each slot in your system. You'll probably have to open the computer's case to determine which cards are in which slots. If necessary, have an expert do this for you.

Slot 1: _____   Slot 5: _____

Slot 2: _____   Slot 6:_____

Slot 3: _____   Slot 7:_____

Slot 4: _____   Slot 8:_____

PERIPHERALS

Enter information about the peripherals attached to your computer. Specify brand names, compatibilities, memory installed, or any other important information.

Printer: _____

Printer: _____

Tape drive: _____

Network: _____

Modem: _____

Scanner: _____

CD-ROM drive: _____

Mouse: _____

Joystick: _____

Other: _____

Other: _____

Other: _____

CMOS MEMORY

The following information pertains to a PC/AT-level system's CMOS memory. Use your PC's Setup program or special key combinations to access the CMOS memory. Enter the proper values in the following sections. (If the category doesn't exist in your Setup program, skip this section.)

Conventional memory: _____

Extended memory: _____

Expanded memory: _____

Primary disk drive: _____ Secondary disk drive: _____

Type of primary hard-disk drive: _____

Type of secondary hard-disk drive: _____

Math coprocessor: _____

Shadow memory: _____

Video/monitor: _____

CONFIG.SYS AND AUTOEXEC.BAT

In addition to the information in this worksheet, it's a good idea to have a printed copy of your CONFIG.SYS and AUTOEXEC.BAT files. Follow these steps:

1. Enter

```
C> copy c:\config.sys prn
```

To eject a page from your printer, use this command:

```
C> echo ^L > prn
```

That's a Ctrl+L character (^L)—*not* the caret and L characters. This sends the form-feed character, ASCII 12, to the printer.

2. Enter

```
C> copy c:\autoexec.bat prn
```

And if you need to eject that page from the printer, use the Echo command again:

```
C> echo ^L > prn
```

Remember to print new copies of CONFIG.SYS and AUTOEXEC.BAT whenever you modify them.

Appendix B

Error Messages

This appendix lists various MS-DOS error messages and gives their descriptions and possible solutions. Refer to the Troubleshooting Guide in Chapter 11 for more information about dealing with common PC problems.

xxx lost allocation units found in *xxx* chains

Chkdsk generates this error message, which indicates that the FAT contains used sectors and no file is claiming ownership of them. You can easily convert these *lost allocation units* (sometimes called *lost clusters*) into files by using the *chkdsk /f* command and answering Y at the prompt. Refer to Chapter 11 for more information.

Abort, Retry, Ignore, Fail?

This prompt is preceded by an MS-DOS error message and signifies either a read or write error to an MS-DOS device, usually a disk drive or a communications port. Your first response should be to press R for Retry. Pressing A for Abort cancels the command. Refer to Chapter 11 for more information.

Access denied

An attempt has been made to overwrite or modify a read-only file. The file's read-only attribute can be changed using the Attrib command; however, it's a good idea to leave the attribute alone because read-only protection is one of MS-DOS's few file-protection features. Refer to "Protecting Vital Files" in Chapter 6 for additional information.

Bad command or file name

MS-DOS doesn't understand the command you typed at the prompt. It could be due to a typo, a missing command, a program not on the search path, and so on. Correct any typing mistakes, or refer to Chapter 11 for information about locating lost programs.

Bad or missing Command Interpreter

MS-DOS cannot locate the file COMMAND.COM (the command interpreter) and cannot start the computer. The Shell configuration command might be specifying an incorrect location for COMMAND.COM, or something might have deleted the COMMAND.COM file from your disk. Try booting your computer with another disk, or refer to Chapter 11 for more information.

Bad partition table

MS-DOS cannot find the hard-disk drive's partition table. This is usually a sign that the hard-disk drive hasn't been initialized by Fdisk to run under MS-DOS. Use Fdisk to prepare the disk for use. Refer to "Check the Partition Table" in Chapter 8.

Cannot find system files

The disk isn't a boot disk; MS-DOS cannot locate one or more of the system files it needs to start: IO.SYS, MSDOS.SYS, or COMMAND.COM. (In PC-DOS, these files are called IBMBIO.COM, IBMDOS.COM, and COMMAND.COM.) Boot from another disk and then try the Sys command on the drive to move the system files to it. Refer to Chapter 11.

Cannot load COMMAND, system halted
Cannot start COMMAND, exiting

This message typically occurs after your computer has started and after you've quit a program to return to MS-DOS. Something might have damaged memory or the COMMAND.COM file, and MS-DOS cannot load the command interpreter. Reset and then check your system's COMSPEC variable to be sure it properly reflects the location of COMMAND.COM. You might also need to copy a fresh COMMAND.COM file to the disk from another boot disk.

Divide overflow

An application has attempted to divide a number by 0. MS-DOS catches this hardware error and then returns you to the MS-DOS prompt. First, try the program again to be sure the problem is consistent. If so, you might

want to reinstall that program from a fresh copy or a backup disk. If the
problem persists, alert the software developer about the situation.

Duplicate file name or file not found

This message is caused when you use the Rename (or Ren) command to
give a file a new name and another file in the same directory already has
that name. Select a new name for the file, or rename the file that already
has the name.

File creation error

MS-DOS cannot create the file for a number of reasons: The disk doesn't
have room for the file; a read-only, hidden, or system file with that name
already exists; or, most commonly, the disk is write-protected. Try using
another disk or saving the file to another location.

File not found

MS-DOS cannot locate the file you've specified. Check your spelling and
be sure you're logged to the proper drive or directory. Refer to Chapter 11
for additional information.

General failure

Typically this error occurs when you try to access an unformatted disk or
when a floppy disk isn't properly inserted into the drive. Replace the disk
with a formatted one or format an unformatted disk using the Format command. For hard-disk drives, this is a sign of an uninitiated drive; refer to
Chapters 8 and 11 for additional information.

Insufficient disk space

The disk is full. This message occurs when a disk physically cannot hold
any more files, or when you fill the root directory with the maximum
number of entries (512). Try another disk to hold your files, or delete files
from the disk to make room for new ones. If the root directory is full, refer
to Chapter 11 for cleanup techniques.

Internal stack overflow/System halted

MS-DOS cannot continue because its stack area (an internal storage location) is full. Reset your system, and then modify CONFIG.SYS with the Stacks configuration command: If you have *stacks=0,0*, remove that line so that MS-DOS will use its default value. Otherwise, setting *stacks=9,128* is a good option.

Invalid COMMAND.COM

This message occurs when COMMAND.COM has become damaged, in which case you should replace it with a fresh copy from a backup disk, or when the file you have specified using the Shell configuration command isn't really the COMMAND.COM file. Check the Shell configuration command and be sure it points to a true copy of COMMAND.COM. If not, copy COMMAND.COM from a boot disk to the proper location on your hard-disk drive.

Invalid media or Track 0 bad - disk unusable

MS-DOS cannot format the disk. If you have a bulk eraser, completely zap the disk and try to format it again. For more information, see Chapter 3.

Invalid media type

This is a hard-disk drive error that typically indicates a non–MS-DOS hard-disk drive, or a hard-disk drive that hasn't been set up with Fdisk or formatted. Set up the disk using Fdisk and then format it according to the instructions in Chapter 8. If this message occurs when the disk is a floppy disk, the disk is only partially formatted; use the Format command to reformat the disk.

Out of environment space

Produced by the Set command, or any utility that accesses the environment, this error message means that there's no more room left to store environment variables. You can use the Set command to delete variables no longer needed: *set variable=* (with nothing following the equal sign). Or you can create a larger environment using the Shell configuration command to load COMMAND.COM. Specify the /P and /E switches.

Follow the /E switch with a colon and the size of the environment in bytes. For example:

```
shell=c:\ms-dos\command.com /p /e:512
```

In this example, a 512-byte environment is created.

Packed file corrupt

This error message is part of an EXE file, put there by the *linker* program that's used to create EXE files. (Programmers use linkers to chain together the separate elements of a program file.) When an EXE file attempts to load below the first 64-KB boundary in a PC, this message occurs. That's allowable under MS-DOS 5, but not according to the program. To get things right, use the Loadfix command: Put *loadfix* (and a space) before the program's name at the MS-DOS prompt.

Sector not found

This message is caused by a bad sector on disk or another disk problem. Third-party utilities can locate the bad sector, rescue data from it, and mark it as bad in the FAT. This prevents other programs from using the same sector and allows you to continue using your disk. Under MS-DOS, your only recourse is to back up the drive as best as you can and then re-format it. The Format program will locate and mark the bad sector. Or you can rename the file something like BADSECT.1, and make the file read-only and invisible using the attrib command (*attrib +h +r badsect.1*). This "locks out" the bad sector from future use, but creates an ugly wart-file in the middle of your drive. It's a livable but clumsy solution.

Appendix C

Emergency Boot Disk Contents & Suggestions

Complete details about the Emergency Boot Disk are given in Chapter 5. This appendix lists the files recommended for the Emergency Boot Disk (other than the system files required to make a disk a boot disk):

BACKUP.EXE	MIRROR.COM
CHKDSK.EXE	PARTNSAV.FIL
DEBUG.EXE	RESTORE.EXE
EDLIN.EXE	SYS.COM
FDISK.EXE	UNDELETE.EXE
FORMAT.COM	UNFORMAT.COM
MEM.EXE	

Be sure to create custom CONFIG.SYS and AUTOEXEC.BAT files. You might also consider copying these other files to the disk:

BIGLIST	HIMEM.SYS
BIGLIST.BAT	VCHECK.BAT
DOSKEY.COM	

In addition to these files, put any third-party utilities you favor on the Emergency Boot Disk.

If you're using a third-party backup program, you should consider creating a Backup/Restore Disk containing your backup program's Restore command plus any directory or catalog files required for the restoration process.

You can also create additional, specialized disks. For example, create one for a favorite third-party utility, create a custom diagnostic disk, and so on.

Index

Dan Gookin

Dan Gookin is a free-lance writer specializing in books and articles about MS-DOS and IBM personal computers. Someday he hopes to do some fiction. Someday. Until then, Dan lives in the drizzly Northwest and dreams of being baked inside a huge Grand Central Bakery rosemary peasant bun so he can eat his way out using only a stick of butter. He is also the author of the *Microsoft Guide to Managing Memory with DOS 5*.

The manuscript for this book was prepared and submitted to Microsoft Press in electronic form. Text files were processed and formatted using Microsoft Word.

Principal word processor: Christina Smith
Principal proofreader: Polly Fox Urban
Principal typographer: Zaafar Hasnain
Interior text designer: Kim Eggleston
Principal illustrator: Margarite Hargrave
Cover designer: Rebecca Geisler
Cover color separator: Color Service

Text composition by Online Press in Times Roman with display type in Futura Heavy, using Ventura Publisher and the Linotronic 300 laser imagesetter.

Printed on recycled paper stock.

The Authorized Editions on DOS 5

RUNNING MS-DOS® 5th ed.
Van Wolverton

Now updated to include DOS 5, RUNNING MS-DOS, 5th ed., is the ideal book for all levels—from novices to advanced DOS users. For novices, this is a solid introduction to basic DOS concepts and applications. For seasoned users this book provides all you need to achieve DOS mastery—precise, real-world examples, thoughtful discussions, and understandable descriptions. The author addresses the exciting improvements in DOS 5 while providing in-depth coverage of every major version of DOS. You'll discover how to

- increase your productivity with the DOS shell
- use the new sort and search capabilities of the Directory command
- create keyboard macros and batch files with the Doskey utility
- edit text files with the new menu-based MS-DOS editor

Also included is a completely revised and updated command reference—an invaluable resource for *every* DOS user. Two million readers can't be wrong. This is the most popular book on DOS available.
592 pages, softcover $24.95   ($31.95 Canada)

SUPERCHARGING MS-DOS® 3rd ed.
Van Wolverton and Dan Gookin

When you're ready for more—turn to SUPERCHARGING MS-DOS. This sequel to *Running MS-DOS* provides tips for intermediate to advanced business users on maximizing the power of DOS. Updated for DOS 5, the authors have packed the book with proven strategies for

- maximizing productivity with DOS
- using DOS with Windows
- managing memory effectively
- using Epson and HP LaserJet printers

You'll also find scores of new batch files and examples to help you get the most out of DOS. Move up to power user with this great resource!
425 pages, softcover $24.95   ($32.95 Canada)

THE MICROSOFT® GUIDE TO MANAGING MEMORY WITH DOS 5
Dan Gookin

One of the most significant features of DOS 5 is its ability to use extended and expanded memory to effectively shatter the 640K barrier. If you're a beginning to intermediate DOS 5 user this official guide provides clear information on how this is done. Here's what's covered:

- the basics of memory—what is it and how your computer uses it
- the differences between conventional, extended, and expanded memory—in clear English
- buying, installing, and using RAM chips and memory boards
- tips on running the Windows environment more efficiently with DOS 5
- and much more

A great little book packed with advice.
208 pages, softcover $14.95   ($19.95 Canada)

Microsoft Press books are available wherever quality computer books are sold.
*Or call **1-800-MSPRESS** for ordering information or placing credit card orders.**
*Please refer to **BBK** when placing your order. Prices subject to change.*

* In Canada, contact Macmillan Canada, Attn: Microsoft Press Dept., 164 Commander Blvd., Agincourt, Ontario, Canada
M1S 3C7, or call (416) 293-8141.

In the U.K., contact Microsoft Press, 27 Wrights Lane, London W8 5TZ.

More Great Resources from Microsoft Press

RUNNING WINDOWS™ 3.1, 3rd ed.

Craig Stinson

"RUNNING WINDOWS does not skirt a subject, but instead dives right in...The text is clear and concise...Its detailed explanations will save you much more time than it takes to read it." **PC Magazine**

Build your confidence and enhance your productivity with Microsoft Windows, quickly and easily, using this hands-on introduction. This Microsoft-authorized edition—for new as well as experienced Windows users—is completely updated and expanded to cover all the new exciting features of version 3.1. You'll find a successful combination of step-by-step tutorials, helpful screen illustrations, expert tips, and real-world examples. Learn how to install and start using Windows 3.1, how to use applications with Windows, and how to maximize Windows performance.

608 pages, softcover $27.95   ($37.95 Canada)   Available April 1992

WINDOWS™ 3.1 COMPANION

The Cobb Group: Lori L. Lorenz and R. Michael O'Mara with Russell Borland

"Covers the basics thoroughly...An excellent reference featuring dozens of live examples. **PC Magazine**

This up-to-date resource thoroughly covers Windows version 3.1—everything from installing and starting Windows to using all of its features—plus a wealth of tips and tricks to show you how to use Windows more efficiently. Novices will value the book for its step-by-step tutorials and great examples; more experienced users will turn to it again and again for its expert advice, unique tips, and useful information. The authors also detail the features and use of Windows' Program Manager, File Manager, and Print Manager so that you'll be able to move smoothly and efficiently through Windows, control the environment, and easily manage files, disks, and printers.

550 pages, softcover $27.95   ($37.95 Canada)

MICROSOFT® PRESS COMPUTER DICTIONARY
The Comprehensive Standard for Business, School, Library, and Home

This is a rich and comprehensive dictionary for those who work with with microcomputers but who are not computer professionals. It's perfect for students, secretaries, managers, and business professionals—anyone who wants a quick and reliable guide to microcomputer terms and phrases. Wide-ranging in scope, it covers memory management, desktop publishing, applications, programming, hardware, graphics, system software, communications, printing, networks, electronics, data storage, computer-industry slang, and more. Each entry is concise yet truly informative. Drawings, diagrams, and other graphics enhance many definitions and provide additional detail. All entries are fully cross-referenced to provide supplementary information and invite further exploration. The MICROSOFT PRESS COMPUTER DICTIONARY was compiled by a distinguished board of advisors drawn from the computer, business, and academic communities.

400 pages, softcover $19.95   ($24.95 Canada)

Microsoft Press books are available wherever quality computer books are sold.
*Or call **1-800-MSPRESS** for ordering information or placing credit card orders.**
*Please refer to **BBK** when placing your order. Prices subject to change.*

* In Canada, contact Macmillan Canada, Attn: Microsoft Press Dept., 164 Commander Blvd., Agincourt, Ontario, Canada M1S 3C7, or call (416) 293-8141.

In the U.K., contact Microsoft Press, 27 Wrights Lane, London W8 5TZ.